Cities in Crisis

The Christian Response

Cities In Crisis

THE CHRISTIAN RESPONSE

by Dennis Clark

SHEED & WARD - *New York*

Contents

ACKNOWLEDGMENT

The author wishes to thank the editors of *Ave Maria* for their permission to reprint material which first appeared in their pages.

Introduction

THE CITY is the earth's most striking symbol of man's lordship over nature. It is in the city that man faces the test of his faith and abilities in the most compelling and exacting way. In the urban community man must contend for the control of the earth's fruit and of his own works. The power of the city indicts his humility; its complexity taxes his knowledge and the abundance of human construction tempts him to delusion. He cannot rely upon the natural rhythm of agrarian life to guide him, for the urban tempo is too much an echo of his own volatile pulse. This is the most extraordinary feature of urban life: *it is the ultimate social arena where man faces his most comprehensive and profound ordeal to preserve the integrity of his spiritual life in community.*

For most of its history, the city has been a religiously orientated environment. Man's religious requirements have led him consistently to adapt the city as a form of social organization for religious ends. The ancient city and the medieval city were clearly committed to religious orthodoxies. If there have been periods when this commitment was less formal, then it was so largely because the religious spirit was either patently assumed or thoroughly implicit in the fabric of municipal life. Urban man, until very recently, has assumed that the bonds of civic life were consecrated to religious ideals or in some way ratified by a general religious assent among the populace. Modern man, however, has rejected this tradition and built his cities upon the premises of humanist and secular ideologies.

Although she has struggled to maintain the Christian image of man amid the distortions and excesses of modern urbanism, the Catholic Church has been hampered in her mission by the frequent hesitation and almost epidemic inertia of her adherents, the ascendancy of her opponents and the swiftness of machine-driven social change.

Certain realizations should make this fact clear. Christian man, the *alter Christus,* has not yet really made his ideals effective in the power structure of the technical city. Despite the immense effort and sacrifice of the Church in founding and maintaining urban parishes, Christianity has not yet squarely faced or truly come to grips with the forces and groups ruling city life. Many of the social evils indicted in the encyclicals *Rerum Novarum* (1891) and *Quadragesimo Anno* (1931) remain virtually unaffected by Christian reforms. The economic system responsible for the cities retains its secular alignment while the weakly presented Christian Gospel of service and sanctification seems to be smothered in the output of countless products for a privileged minority of the industrial regions.

Much of the lay apostolate today is not based on any program or deployment of resources, but rather upon the needs which have accidentally been presented in the historical course of events. Whatever may be said of this development in its aspects of democracy and enthusiasm, the question of what problems have real and urgent precedence for Catholicism in the social order has not been clearly presented.

What is the mission of Christians with respect to the social problem of the modern city? What are the tasks of the apostolate in relation to it? The first task is obviously to gain a knowledge of it. There is a staggering work of analysis to be performed before we can separate the wise from the foolish elements in the urban environment.

This brief book is intended as a survey of some of the major problems of Christian religious life in the modern urban environment. The necessity of examining Christian conduct in a time of swift social change and urban growth has prompted many of the studies cited in these pages. It is hoped that if some of the difficulties which Christians face in city life are specified, the individual will be helped to an awareness of his personal religious situation and a more intelligent service of the community. It is a way of understanding the concrete circumstances in which the Incarnation must take place in the contemporary world. Christians must adopt a more informed approach to modern city life not only for the sake of political and social ends, but because of specific religious needs and opportunities. As Christ entered the great city of His nation to teach, pray, cure, sacrifice and redeem, so He must enter our cities.

These chapters are also an effort to encourage a fuller

inquiry into the religious implications of urbanism. The presentation is not a definitive one, but is conceived as a summary of the religious and social issues at stake. The body of the book is concerned with the metropolitan life produced by modern technology. In order to provide some historical orientation, so that the truly radical character of modern urban development can be appreciated, an appendix treating the city life of the past has been placed at the end of the book.

Cities in Crisis

The Christian Response

1. Revolutionary Cities

1

The Revolutionary City

FOR THE past three centuries the city as a form of community life has seemed to be inundated like an Atlantis in the tides of social history. Great waves of population, technical audacity and cultural changes have washed over the city, gathering momentum until the city's features, its purpose and form were obscured by the interaction of these influences. Then the city rose from its immersion, still seething with new forces, but transformed, powerful and immense. The Atlantis of modern urbanism is gradually emerging with a form of its own to dominate the life of the modern world.

The forces of technology and industry in the West have built a way of life which is new to the history of man. The momentous nature of the change is all but overpowering. For all of previous history the life of man was attuned to agrarian cycles, the impulses of which were felt even within the walls of the ancient cities. Human culture was impregnated with the quality and tone of this ruralism, notwithstanding the increasingly important role of the cities in cultural development. Then, within the passage of three centuries, the orbit was reversed and the tempo of Western man's most important movements emanated from the increasingly vibrant centers of urban life.

The advent of the revolutionary city has brought a new way of life to the ordinary man. In the age which preceded the last three centuries the great majority of men were seldom directly involved in revolutionary movements. Revolutions were made by minorities, by cabals and groups of zealots. For most men life continued in the same pattern, periodically interrupted by famine or war, perhaps made more or less tolerable by the policies of the group in power. Any change in the class in power or shift in policy was moderated by the limitations of technology and the orthodox codes and religions of conservative societies. The common person, Everyman, was only occasionally brought into the scene when a revolution was in the making, and even then was admitted grudgingly. In modern times, however, Everyone—the mass city inhabitant—is an energetic protagonist of social revolution. Through the media of popular sovereignty, the principle of majority rule, general literacy, mass communication and rising standards of living, Everyone has become directly involved in the successive changes encompassed in the urban way of life.

This breadth of collaboration in social change does not alter the fact that creative elites are still the critical agents of social change. These elites have had their power tremendously augmented by technical and political innovations. The transformations brought about by the "revolt of the masses" have been matched by the strength of institutions directed by business and scientific elites.

These elites are partisans of change; even their conservative segments are committed to popular sovereignty in some form, and to large-scale industrialism and urban expansion. Thus, the fluid quality of modern urbanism derives not only from the rapid growth and movement of population and the active engagement of that population in social decisions, but also from the inventive elite which arbitrates the social affairs of technological societies.

The conditions which have produced revolutionary urbanism are not conditions of community form, so much as they are flexible systems or trends which mediate between forms or serve as catalysts for changes of structure. The technology and political democracy of the West constantly minister to further change, and within the framework of these two cultural vehicles, the social combustion of population rise, political reform and economic development continues. The setting which urbanism provides for this process has never yet been clearly defined. The definition of the modern city is made most difficult because of the flexibility inherent in revolutionary urbanism. Yet, it is possible to isolate certain of its features: its physical giantism, the high degree of specialization of labor, the density, mobility and heterogeneity of its population, its constant technical and cultural innovations. In this chapter we shall try to refine some of these categories with a view to discovering just how they produce the quality of successive revolution in modern urbanism. We shall examine the population, technology, movement and social relations of the industrial metropolis. Then we shall note some of the religious implications of these elements.

OVER-POPULATION OF CITIES

The industrialized city of the 20th century is above all a place of large and often densely distributed population; the city is the pre-eminent social response to the phenomenal growth of population in modern times. In the last three hundred years the population of the world has quadrupled, a rate of growth estimated to be almost sixty times that which existed until 1650 A.D., and the next thirty years may see a world population increase of 50 per cent over the present 2,400 million figure.[1] This growth is perhaps the primary factor accounting for the revolutionary expansion and alteration of urban forms. In accommodating this vast population, the city has become plastic, some would even say deformed. It is not that a city or some cities have failed to plan for and assimilate in orderly fashion new population, but rather that the city *per se* as an organism of social life has been rendered elastic by the proliferation of life and activity on every side.

The historical character of urban life has been fundamentally altered by the multiplication of the population, and the effects of population growth in the future may be even more extraordinary and far-reaching. One authority states:

If present trends are projected the majority [of urbanites] are likely to find themselves living in vast metropolitan centers, some of them reaching a size entirely unprecedented. . . . Of the twenty-five largest cities in the world, according to the latest figures available in 1959, twelve were in Japan, China, India, Africa and Latin America. And at least eight additional cities in India and Southeast Asia are rapidly pushing into this category. . . . And the wave of urbanization is just beginning.[2]

This is a global development, and all of our comment about American conditions should be related to this fact.

The population expansion of the world foreshadows an urbanized age in which great social wisdom will be imperative. The density of population in modern cities is a problem which harries the expert on city life incessantly, and its economic, geographic, cultural and psychological ramifications are staggering. In the face of accelerating population increases, experts warn that without a limitation on the maximum size and population of the city, effective planning will be impossible. The revolutionary city has been so elastic that it cannot plan even to distribute population according to some order to obtain tolerable internal conditions.

The problem of population density underlies all other urban social problems. The concentration of great numbers of people in small spaces makes constant change necessary: wear and tear on buildings and utilities brings about continuous physical renovation; the diversities of a mass population make innovation and specialized services profitable; the boredom which wells up in the face of the mass-communication stereotypes directed at large populations induces an eager search for novelty. The intensive interaction of individuals and groups in high-density areas of itself gives rise to countless forms of movement. This social movement is often pathological, or at least irrational. The manipulation of nationalist throngs by Hitler and Mussolini revealed in a terrible way the irascible and

primitive forces resident in a dense populace and dramatized the fact that Western cities are often more densely
packed than the traditional "teeming cities of Asia." Paris
has 108 persons per gross acre, for instance, while Jakarta
has only 12 persons and Cairo 6 to an acre.[3] The physical
ugliness and grossness brought about by this kind of population density are obvious; the psychological ravages and
the assault against human dignity caused by such concentration mean a shocking debasement in both the biological and intellectual orders.

THE LACK OF SOCIAL CONSENSUS

Another charateristic of the population of the revolutionary city is its heterogeneity. From tribe and village,
farm and plain, from numerous nations and dissimilar
groups in thousands of widely scattered communities
come the people of the city. They now live in the same
place, often trying to continue their old ways of life amid
the bewildering polyglot scenes of the urban center.[4] This
diversity was loosely federated by the industrial system
itself and by political expediency. Various ethnic and class
ghettos existed in close proximity with a mutual sense of
the need for survival. The failure of ethnic groups to perpetuate their social systems and mores and make them
permanent features in the American urban scene has, paradoxically, been another cause of change in the revolutionary city. The demands of each newly arrived
population group, their failure in turn to perpetuate themselves as an enduring minority enclave, and their adoption
of local urban customs have formed a cycle of group as-
similation which has helped to animate the great city.

The cultural adjustment and interplay of the mixed population of the modern city foster a cosmopolitan tolerance of differences. These differences are contained below the level of professional and elite life, where an accepted minimal code of eclectic standards holds sway. On the primary levels of social life the differences at times approach anarchic divergence. The bond of social life does not arise from internal belief so much as from external suggestion. The problem of obtaining social solidarity among urbanites on this primary level is one which has long troubled social thinkers. The demands of a democratic system make especially necessary an informed and ready consensus and a public solidarity. De Tocqueville's dictum that "a society can exist only when a great number of men consider a great number of things from the same point of view" has been many times reaffirmed from the vantage point of the urban sociologist. Louis Wirth, for example, writes in strong terms of the importance of common experience and agreement among urbanites.[5] The volatile and heterogeneous character of the urban way of life makes the achievement of a consensus on public policy and local community standards an elusive, tentative and increasingly precious goal. It is clear that the lack of social consensus in the urban environment is one more condition favoring urban social revolution.

THE TECHNOLOGICAL ORDER

The modern city is also molded by its industrial and commercial technology. The cultural innovations brought by the mechanical and chemical sciences in the last three centuries have not only sustained the life of vastly increased populations, but have added a new dimension of adequacy and comfort to the social life of millions. That this technical bounty has quickened the inventive instincts of man and whetted the appetite of society for more technical goods is obvious. This continuous technical innovation has provided the modern city with skills and machines which expedite further changes in urban life. The material standard of living made possible by technology has attracted immigrant populations to the city. The "master institutions" of the technological order, the business and commercial aggregates, dictate to a considerable extent the use of time, space and energy in urban centers and formulate the prevailing standards by which success is measured. By making, in Arnold Toynbee's phrase, "the ideal of welfare for all a practical objective instead of a Utopian dream," it has changed one of society's basic attitudes. Under welfare state auspices, flexible policies of economic experiment and regulation underwrite and facilitate the achievements of urban technology, with its cycles, mass production and marketing methods and ceaseless preoccupation with novelty.[6]

The productive capacity and material abundance which make this complex urban life possible have been purchased at a certain cultural cost. One of the prices paid for material success in urban society has been the sacrifice of broad cultural facility and experience on the part of the citizen. The generalized principles of judgment and education which were the standards of cultural reference for centuries in the Western cities were sacrificed to the needs of intensive exploitation of technical advantages. Specialization was demanded of the urbanite, and specialization was achieved. In countless endeavors, tasks were isolated and perfected, multiplying the number of occupations and adding to the continuous variation of city life. Thus specialization has been one of the primary ways in which technology has occasioned civic change.

There are today many misgivings about this entire process. One pessimistic commentator states:

Never before have men made relatively greater progress in the rational control of physical force or relatively less in rational control of social relations. The fundamental reason for this discrepancy is clear: it is that forces of nature have been discovered and applied by a few exceptional individuals, whereas every effort to ameliorate human relations has been frustrated by the fact that society cannot be transformed without the compliance of the untutored masses.[7]

The dilemma of the specialist struggling to relate his achievements to the "popular mind" or to thousands of persons who are specialists in something else is evident. This dilemma is critical in an urban environment, where technology and social relations are inextricably entangled.

Another facet of technical achievement which is also an identifying characteristic of the modern city is the mark of physical giantism. Modern technicians think in terms of colossal structures; the skyscraper is a kind of apotheosis of physical exorbitance. The new-found command of resources and techniques in the 19th century led the modern architect and engineer to indulge in experimental and at times capricious feats of massive construction. These feats became models and established a building cult in the first half of the 20th century which attained a place in the economic order. Railroad stations, public buildings, factories and residential buildings were built on a tremendous scale. The overwhelming size of physical structures in many modern cities dwarfs the social life which goes on within them and subjects it to crude influences.

All of the features of the modern city which we have cited as characteristic must be considered in relation to one another. The interplay of these factors in the urban environment has produced a process of social balance and movement.

URBAN WAYS OF LIFE: THE INDUSTRIAL AREA,

    SLUM AND SUBURB

Within the great city there are three orbits, or ways of life: the commercial-industrial orbit and two orbits based upon residential conditions, the slum and the suburb. Perhaps a better term to describe these three areas of activity would be to call them behavior systems. All of them have been amply scrutinized from a secular point of view in recent years.[8]

The first of these spheres—the maze of companies, unions, systems and ideas which make up the commercial-industrial complex—has largely shaped the policies directing the urban environment. This system has a distinctly secular, pragmatic and utilitarian orientation. It has smothered the privileged populations of the industrialized regions with its output of countless products, and in its behalf the resources of the earth have been exploited.

The second great social sphere of the revolutionary city is the slum, the province of the poor, the rejected, the afflicted. In city after city the bestial conditions of slum life continue to defy community efforts to restore human standards. Social and family disorganization, crime, exploitation, decayed housing and chaotic misuse of land and resources make life in these areas virtually intolerable. City authorities shake their heads at the multiplied tragedies in the slum which threaten to undermine the financial and social life of the industrial cities, but apathy, cynicism, race prejudice and selfishness prevail against the municipal good, and the slum way of life continues.

At the other end of the social scale from the slum is the third orbit of the revolutionary city, the suburb. The suburb has acted as a social shock absorber for urbanism. It is to the suburbs that people have gone to repair their nerves, their reputations and their family life after whirling about in the vortex of urban existence. The comfort of the suburb has cushioned the shock of life in the big city—the daily waves of tension and agitation which the city generates are lost in the domestic propriety of the hinterland. Census Bureau figures show that the suburbs account for the overwhelmingly greater part of metropolitan growth in recent years. Those who can, seek a more humane and tempered life in developments beyond the city limits, notwithstanding an inescapable knowledge of the shortcomings of suburbia.

The revolutionary city has extended its orbits so far that in some locations one huge urban area merges with another. Thus a regional amalgamation of social resources is replacing the traditional form of city organization. This regionalism may eventually be of as great social significance as the cities themselves, recasting the life and boundaries of states and even nations. Regionalism may be the basis for a new organization of political and economic life.[9]

This unprecedented concentration of people and technical development is dramatized in the world of social relations by equally novel departures from historic ways of life. The changes in social patterns brought about by industrial urbanism affect every social unit from the primary group level to the ultimate levels of human organization. The scope of these changes has been great enough to dislocate the transmission of culture. In literature and the arts, where the most significant comment upon human affairs is made, this is not simply a matter of revolt against traditional literary and artistic techniques. The process of intellectual communication itself has been assaulted by the whirlwind pace of social development.

THE ARTISTS' VIEW

"What is the City?" we ask the interpreters of social events, the artists and the men who have the power of artistic insight and definition. The answer lacks substantive meaning and structure. They perceive no form, intent or organization, but rather a concourse, a massing, a mystical virulence and motion. Baudelaire describes a 19th century city:

> Ant hill city, city full of dreams,
> Where the specter in broad daylight accosts the passerby,
> Everywhere mysteries flow like sap
> In the narrow arteries of the powerful Colossus.[10]

Descriptions such as the following by Thomas Wolfe capture the seething spiritual restlessness of the metropolitan people:

The city was their stony-hearted mother, and from her breast they had drawn a bitter nurture. Born to brick and asphalt, to crowded tenements and swarming streets, stunned into sleep as children beneath the sudden slamming racket of the elevated trains, taught to fight, to menace, and to struggle in a world of savage violence and incessant din, they had the city's qualities stamped into their flesh and movements, distilled through all their tissues, etched with the city's acid into their tongue and brain and vision. . . . Their pulse beat with the furious rhythm of the city's stroke; ready in an instant with a curse; metallic clangors sounded from their twisted lips, and their hearts were filled with a dark, immense and secret pride.[11]

T. S. Eliot writes of the social instability of modern urban life:

Though you have shelters and institutions,
Precarious lodgings while the rent is paid,
Subsiding basements where the rat breeds,
Or sanitary dwellings with numbered doors,
Or a house a little better than your neighbors:
When the Stranger says, "What is the meaning of this city?"
"Do you huddle close together because you love one another?"
What will you answer? "We all dwell together
To make money from each other" or "This is a community"?[12]

Works like Theodore Dreiser's *Sister Carrie,* James T. Farrell's Lonigan trilogy and Arthur Miller's *Death of a Salesman* are all documents of social insight. Bitterly ironic, grossly realistic, they are set against an urban background which lacks either clear form or spiritual coherence. Haunted by images—visual and aural, incessant and ubiquitous—the urban man perceives film, photograph, recording and display, but the one image necessary for social guidance and comprehension, the image of God, is obscured. Hence, there is no clear social reflection or pattern, but rather a miasma detailed by the artists who breathe in its terrible toxin. Poets like Freidrich Juenger have been led to draw up sombre indictments of the technical city, unredeemed by any recognition of the cogently expressed values and humane possibilities which yet remain in the revolutionary metropolis.[13] We must augment and correct the defective picture of the city induced by these works if we are to obtain an accurate view of the condition of the Christian community in the revolutionary city. James Joyce in his *Ulysses* is a brilliant representative of the urban artist stretching the very bounds of intellectual comprehension and intelligibility to embrace the flashing mazes of modern city life. *Ulysses* is the last great book of the city: its protagonist, a homeless man of the city, wanders almost dazedly through the perpetual stimulation of concentrated social life.

SOCIAL RELATIONS:

ASSOCIATION AND ISOLATION

The sociologist and historian are also preoccupied with the unique character of social relations in the 20th century technical city. To a greater degree than ever before the life of the ordinary man is taken up with what are called secondary groups. These groups are distinguished from the immemorial primary groups which are based on kinship or immediate residential and friendship association. Secondary groups are based upon more remote affiliation, such as sports clubs, consumer groups, adult education groups. Sociologist Georg Simmel noted the prevalence of these groups in modern life in the early days of formal sociology. This kind of dominant secondary social organization has tended to weaken the fibre of social life and to substitute explicit political control for tacit social control.

The citizen is faced with a complexity in social relations which makes civic responsibility especially difficult for him. His institutions are made vulnerable by the weight of detail and bureaucratic requirements. Even Justice Brandeis, a brilliant legalist with an amazingly retentive mind for corporate detail, stated that the complexity of financial and business interrelations outstripped him at his indefatigable best. The jurist, public administrator, journalist or policy maker confronted by the labyrinth of urban organization is overwhelmed by the dilemmas of metropolitan affairs. The formulae and methods for dealing with such complexity have not yet been devised.

In addition to the complexity of social relationships urban life is highly mobile both in terms of space and social status. This physical and social mobility in the city is a unique demonstration of the volatile nature of the new urbanism. The social status of millions of urban citizens is elevated by accessible wealth and relaxed standards of status definition. A considerable proportion of the industrial population is transient; this implies a high degree of both freedom and insecurity. Ceaseless traffic and residential turnover are all part of a cult of mobility which is becoming a folk habit of the urban peoples, with enervating effects. Nor is this movement that of the nomad in which the entire way of life is oriented around the economic necessity of recurrent pilgrimage; the movement of the modern urbanite is like that of the pioneer who must meet conditions as they come.

While there are many convenient aids to movement, the social techniques to facilitate movement have not been developed except in the broadest and most legalistic sense. Immigration laws, voter and property transfers and school transfers help to form a minimal process for family movements, but the individualist attitudes of the urban milieu and the absence of social cohesion at the primary level make difficult the refinement of basic codes to guide mobility. Hence, in this atmosphere groups of new workers, bourgeois and elite, take shape, shift and are superseded in an almost whimsical fashion in the great city. The mobility which animates the great city has not only caused an expansion of urban boundaries, but is causing legal changes and programs of continuous capital inventory and planning which accept high mobility as the premise of urban government and conservation.

All of these conditions impart to life in the revolutionary city a vicarious quality. The individual sees life in isolated pieces. The minimal consistency of experience and cohesion of cultural context necessary for the formulation of judgments—whether ethical, aesthetic or utilitarian— is hard to find. Paradoxically, the experience of the urban citizen is constricted by the very extension of possible courses of action. In defense against unassimilable stimulation, the urbanite resorts to apathy or illusion as counterfeits for experience.[14]

Thus, the urbanite in the revolutionary city, cut off from root reality by his social situation, responds weakly to the total challenge of his environment. As a specialist he often responds brilliantly, but as a man, a complete person, he responds miserably or not at all. Only part of the man responds; the individual is baffled. The average man tends neither to participate in city affairs nor to see himself as directly related to national and world issues. He is immersed in giant associations—a corporation, a labor union, a large parish—in which his own position is insignificant. The size, technical character and fluid relationships of revolutionary urbanism have outstripped the ability of our present municipal society to construct humane forms of social transition and control.

Our cities are, then, truly revolutionary. That the developments of which we have spoken have been decisive requires little more substantiation than the obvious testimony of current social patterns. Few things could be more radically different from the life of former ages than the daily round of the urbanite in the technical-industrial city. The sheer extent of modern changes, even without inquiry into their quality, would indicate the decisiveness of the new urban achievement.

The leadership of modern urbanism is in and of itself a revolutionary element. The creative urban elite is highly mobile and interchangeable. Even its objectives are those of alteration. It is keenly experimental and resorts to the tentative constructions of the new social sciences to obtain direction and verification for its activities. The technical-industrial city is revolutionary in its nature and in its significance.[15] It has inaugurated an era of successive revolutions.

It would, of course, be impractical in a study of this kind to attempt to evaluate all of the phases of modern city life. It is only proper, then, to select for examination those subjects which the author judges to be of greatest importance to his reader. These subjects are: first, the characteristics of modern urban life in the United States at various levels of social life; and second, the relation of technical industrial urbanism to the spiritual life and institutions of Christians. We have already begun the examination of the new city's characteristics in this chapter.

The city life of the United States is chosen for examination because it is in this country that the city has attained a special vitality and significance. Because of the productive wealth and ingenuity of American society our cities represent an achievement which has a ramifying international effect. The United States is the most powerful of the modern urbanized nations, and will inevitably have its successes and failures in this new way of life imitated throughout the world.

RELIGIOUS IMPLICATIONS

In evaluating any form of culture we must ultimately ask what kind of influence this culture has upon man's spiritual life. It is appropriate, indeed urgent, that cultural changes be weighed against the effects they have upon man's highest motivations and faculties. For what kinds of spiritual behavior do the cities of our time prepare a man? It will be my purpose to relate this question particularly to the life of American Catholics, since this religious group is, I believe, in a pivotal position with respect to the course of urban affairs. The vision of man to which Catholicism adheres embraces religious and metaphysical postulates which make intelligible even the social tempests of the modern world. The doctrinal completeness, social experience and spiritual vitality of Catholicism give it a unique richness to contribute to historical changes. If the Church is the bearer of the God-life appointed by Christ to guide men to salvation, then surely she must have counsel for men in the tumult of the urban scene. This counsel will be borne out in history. The outlines of Catholic approaches to the new cultural conditions of urbanism, however, have yet to be synthesized for the sincere inquirer.

American Catholics are an overwhelmingly urban group. It is their role to translate their religious life into social reality in an urban setting. In the cities of the United States they represent the largest organized religious body. The relationship of religion and the spiritual life to urbanism will in many ways, I believe, be determined and defined by the actions of this religious group in our changing cities. The Catholic population of the United States is engaged in a singular confrontation: the Christian ideal is being rigorously tested in the unprecedented environment of the "revolutionary city."

Father François Houtart, a Belgian sociologist, has written of the modern city:

Urban life is not merely a demographic concentration . . . it is a transformation of society as a whole. The socialization of human life, the importance of institutions, the depersonalization of man, the disappearance of the role of the local community, the creation of functional spheres, where man is considered as fulfilling a particular function (work, amusement, study) are a few symptoms of urban life. From a religious point of view they present a whole new series of problems to the pastorate and the Christianization of the world. These problems are of the sociological order, and their study requires positive methods. The general development of urban sociology everywhere will help us to see them more clearly.[16]

This comment summarizes the sweeping dimensions of the new urban social world which must be interpreted in terms of man's highest destiny—his religious fulfillment.

NOTES

1. United Nations, Department of Public Information, Press and Publications Bureau, Press Release SOC-1341, April 18, 1952.
2. Catherine Bauer, "The Pattern of Urban Economic Development," *The Annals of the American Academy of Political and Social Science* (May, 1956).
3. *New York Times,* August 30, 1957, "108 to Acre in Paris."
4. The plight of the 19th century immigrants is movingly described by historian Oscar Handlin in *The Uprooted* (Boston: Little Brown & Co., 1951).
5. Louis Wirth, *Community Life and Social Policy* (Chicago: University of Chicago Press, 1956), Chapter 3.
6. Sylvia and Benjamin Selekman, *Power and Morality in a Business Society* (New York: McGraw-Hill Co., 1956). See also J. K. Galbraith, *The Affluent Society* (New York: Houghton-Mifflin Co., 1958).

7. Carl Becker, *Progress and Power* (Stanford, California: Stanford University Press, 1936), p. 91.

8. For the commercial-industrial system see C. W. Mills, *The Power Elite* (New York: Oxford University Press, 1956), especially Chapters 6 and 7, and William H. Whyte, *The Organization Man* (New York: Simon and Schuster, 1956). For the slum see Louis Wirth, *The Ghetto* (Chicago: University of Chicago Press, 1959), and Mabel Walker, *Urban Blight and Slums* (Cambridge: Harvard University Press, 1938). For the suburb see R. A. Seeley, E. W. Sim and D. Loosley, *Crestwood Heights* (New York: Basic Books, Inc., 1956), and William M. Dabriner, ed., *The Suburban Community* (New York G. Putnam and Sons, 1938).

9. H. W. Odum and H. E. Moore, *American Regionalism* (New York: Holt & Co., 1938).

10. Translated by Mary Colum in *From These Roots* (New York: Columbia University Press, 1944), p. 194.

11. Thomas Wolfe, *You Can't Go Home Again* (New York: Grosset & Dunlap, 1934), p. 38.

12. T. S. Eliot, "The Rock," *The Complete Poems and Plays of T. S. Eliot* (New York: Harcourt, Brace and Co., 1952), p. 103.

13. F. G. Juenger, *The Failure of Technology* (Chicago: Henry Regnery Co., 1949).

14. *cf.* Simone Weil, *The Need for Roots* (New York: G. P. Putnam's Sons, 1952).

15. Works like Charles Abrams' *Revolution in Land,* James Burnham's *The Managerial Revolution* and Karl Stern's *The Third Revolution* document various phases of the sweeping changes in modern society. See also John Gillin, "The Applications of Anthropological Knowledge to Modern Mass Society" in *Human Organization* (Winter, 1957), p. 27. "Through the new urbanism social revolution has become a cultural commonplace. As one anthropologist states, 'Not only are modern cultures more heterogeneous than folk and primitive systems of life, but they are also in certain senses less stable. Revolution, whether political, technological, ideological or social, is practically a built-in feature of modern cultures, but on the whole exceedingly rare in the so-called simpler societies, unless the later are in contact with complex civilizations.' I use

the word 'Revolution' to refer to abrupt changes affecting at
least a major section of a culture."

16. François Houtart, "A Sociological Study of the Evolution of
American Catholics," in *Social Compass* (November, 1956),
p. 190.

2. The Urbanite: Eyeless in Gaza

The Image of Man
Physical Effects of Urbanism
Psychological Effects of Urbanism
The Socialization of the Mind
The Normless Attitude
The Threat to Human Freedom

The Urbanite: Eyeless in Gaza

THE IMAGE OF MAN

THE CITY was created to serve man; but in the modern world there is, in a sense, no "man" for the city to serve; there are many men and no generally accepted ideals of the human person. The traditional Western ideal of man as a "rational creature fully considered in all his essential relations" certainly persists, but as a standard of reference in the modern urban scene it has been compromised both theoretically and practically. Not only is the ideal of "rational" man widely repudiated, but all definitions of man which assign a supernatural dimension to his nature are questioned.

If there is no one philosophical view of man gaining wide allegiance in the modern city, events themselves have provided us with summary images which give testimony to the results of the various ideals of man that compete in the urban marketplace. A study of the history of the 20th century provides two striking views of man. One is a nihilist and barbaric concept which permits the treatment of the human person with ruthless expediency; the genocide attempted by Nazi Germany, the slave empire used to build the Soviet industrial machine, the colonial exploitations which produce the materials for much of Western technology are harrowing examples of this view in operation. The second view is one born of the modern passion for scientific success; it is a mystical and excited view of man dedicated to confidence in human abilities, glorifying the fruits of rationality even while decrying reason as a spiritual faculty.

Both of these images derive, ultimately, from philosophies of the person. The nihilist view derives from the subjective interpretation of the human person which became popular in the 19th century, described by Romano Guardini as

Conceived . . . as flowing from roots intrinsic in itself, as shaped in its destiny through its own initiative, personality became . . . something primary and absolute which could not be questioned or doubted. The great personality was looked upon as a man who had to be taken inevitably upon his own terms. Only in the light of his own unique "personality" might one dare to justify the actions of a man. Ethical standards seemed relative when compared to those which genius deserved. This new measure for judging the human act in terms of "personality" was first applied to the extraordinary man; it soon applied for humanity at large.[1]

This interpretation gradually degenerated from one of controlled subjectivity to one of arrant wilfulness and, finally, nihilist bestiality.

The second image is one which exalts man by focusing on his scientific prowess. This image has been termed the "divinization of man" by Pope Pius XII, who described the orientation of the scientific man as one in which the subject is

. . . so convinced of his own power, inclined to measure his stature according to the power of his instruments, his organizations, his weapons, the precision of his calculations, the vastness of his production, of the distance he can reach with his words, his gaze and his influence; this man who speaks at length with pride of an age of easy prosperity as if one had just to reach out a hand for it; who is so sure of himself that he dares all, urged by an insatiable desire to know nature's deepest secrets, to bend its forces to his own will, eager to penetrate in his own person the interplanetary spaces.

(Christmas Message—1955)

This image has its genesis in the cult of the impersonal and the love of objectivity. The severe functionalism of modern architecture, the efficient regularity of the mechanized business world and the neuter mentality sought after in the social sciences are all examples of this extreme and erroneous "objectivity."

These polar images of man coexist in the modern city and could probably be said to be the dominant themes of the urban estimate of the person. The subjectivist view is the more widespread and operative. It is abetted by the entire emphasis of popular culture and mass communications. The celebrities of the urban scene often have its attributes; the man of power, the self-made man, the gifted, erratic man of talent; the extravagant movie queen —all of these types partake of the ideal of successful subjectivity. The concept of high "objectivity" with its eager confidence in scientific achievement is often adhered to as a discipline of life by the creative elite of modern industrial society. The skilled elite continues to hold to this view of man in the face of growing misgivings about utilitarian science as a civilizing agent in society. The beguiling power of the sleek, ingenious maze of "objective" technical creation supports this concept of the human person. Naturally, few people consciously hold either of these concepts. But informal attachment to these interpretations is ubiquitous and active.

These confused estimates of the person have given rise to the position that there is no real relationship between the person and the urban environment. Man and his powers for subjective fulfillment or technical genius are above environmental influences. Is not man at last master of the world through technical achievement? Has he not liberated himself from primitive dependence upon rain and sun, soil and topography so that he can plan his surroundings to maximize freedom and convenience? It is an outlook that is tremendously attractive in its simplicity and its appeal to confidence. Men in planning, administrative and engineering professions where programs are carried out under pressure of time find such a view superficially efficient and untrammelling. The kind of technical endeavor which is so widespread in modern cities, aloof from organic processes and abstracted from primary social situations, is fertile ground for such opinion. Against such a view must be placed all of those insights and studies which account for the subtle interaction between man and his surroundings and affirm the dependence of man in amazingly concrete ways upon the complex features of the urban setting. "The urban landscape we want to improve by our artifacts is in the first place a phenomenon to be understood on a biological basis," says architect Richard Neutra. "We know that the individual is not separable from it. This is not a philosophical thought, but one entirely borne out by current science."[2] Yet even this minimal recognition of the link between urbanism and personality is usually forgotten in the direction of social affairs.

The significance of the city in relation to the person has been probed by studies of social and psychological deviation, and although the relation which urban community life has to the general process of personality formation has not received sufficient study, the effects of urban social experience upon the development, vitality and conduct of the person are generally admitted to be intimate and intensive.[3] Indeed the immense power and stimulation of revolutionary urbanism has so profoundly affected the molding of the human person that some observers contend that a "new man" has arisen in this environment; it is claimed that the new associational type of society has so modified and conditioned the functions and qualities of the human person that a new historical type has been produced, possessed of a novel set of capabilities and deficient in some powers that were resident in the person in past ages.[4] Max Lerner has described an American type formed by an urban environment:

It has been psychologically hardened by innumerable brief encounters—in public schools, on subways and busses, in restaurants, in the course of shopping—which would become intolerable if one did not sheathe oneself against them with a constricted response. It is precocious about money matters and sex, since so many city people grow up in crowded quarters where few things are concealed from them. It is stoical in the face of hardship and the man-made catastrophes of economic life. It is not "urbane" except in the small groups in which one can afford to be generous, but it is much more likely to strip the jungle life of the city down to the nakedness of the human animal. It economizes time with an almost manic earnestness during the hours of business, only to waste it with equally manic intensity during the hours of pleasure and recreation. It lays stress (within limits) on individual traits of personality, on uniqueness in dress and sophistication in taste, on awareness, on the dramatic impact that the individual makes in his brief meetings with others. It has replaced fear by anxiety, and the concern about danger from elemental forces with a vague concern about security, safety, and the opinions of others. What this means is that city living has carried men and women ever further away from their instinctual endowment.[5]

Another view of the effects of technical urbanism on the person sees man cut off from natural ties and social supports, weakened in the face of pathological tendencies and reduced to a forlorn "rabble."[6] Whatever may be the specific judgment of those concerned with the welfare and integrity of the person in urban society, the undeniable and effective relationship between the milieu and the nature of man is verifiable both empirically and philosophically.

In attempting to work out some of the specifics of this relationship, we will use the Scholastic categories and examine first the biological basis of the person, then the faculties of intellect and will.

PHYSICAL EFFECTS OF URBANISM

The integrity of the body and its functions has been the subject not only of social interest, but of actual social regulation throughout history. The revolutionary city introduces unprecedented conditions into the social task of maintaining the biological integrity of the human person. Before the modern era, the eugenic and biological components of the person were largely shaped by impersonal physical conditions; social codes and conscious policies of mating, nutrition and body care were secondary to the influence of climate, food supply and disease. Now this proportion has changed, and it is the consciously constructed social apparatus which has the greatest influence upon biological heritage, particularly that of the city dweller. Medical advances, the abundance of food, shelter and clothing, and humanitarian labor reforms have reduced infant mortality and disease and extended the life span. The revolutionary city has provided conditions in which the human organism has preserved the results of its fertility, achieved fuller growth and obtained immunity from former scourges. Although an increased number of handicapped or weak persons live to maturity, the great majority of the population enjoys a notable degree of physical fitness.

In another way, however, the novel demographic characteristics of the modern city provide a radical biological basis for urban life. High marriage rates, small family size, longer life spans and the sustenance of weaker types make the urbanite more and more dependent upon favorable environmental conditions and less upon biological strength. The wealth of the mechanized cities makes possible the support of parasitic and aged or incompetent life on a vast scale. Even the conditions for the ordinary physical activity necessary for biological health are not present. Hence, the cult of ennui grows and stamina declines. Taken out of its context in the organic world of nature and surrounded by artificial forms of technology, the human organism is altered by whim and mechanized custom. The mere complexity of the response required of the organism in technical-industrial activities is an amazing taxation of the physical and chemical system.

Has the revolutionary city actually weakened man's inherent biological capabilities? There does not appear to be sufficient anthropological knowledge to answer this question satisfactorily. We have seen that certain grave problems have arisen. Reservations about the effect of modern urbanism on the human organism do seem warranted.[7] We do not know, for example, if the biological propagation accounting for mass populations is a pathological condition, carried on in some societies at the expense of a certain order of social relations.

Then too the extension of the physical organism into the areas of sensory and psycho-physical activity is an exceedingly delicate process. It is in this area of the collaboration between body and mind that the hidden effects of the urban environment become apparent. The physical organism has been conditioned in the technical city to patterns of stimulation and enervation which have important repercussions in the realm of neurology and psychology. The emotional life of man in the industrial city is characterized by pronounced oscillations and extremes. Periods of hyperactive tension alternate with periods of extreme indifference. Although the high intensity of emotional life made possible by the concentrated stimulation of the city is one of the factors responsible for the creative potential of the city, it also has its destructive effects. The emotional dynamism of modern urbanism and its achievements have not been sustained without great attrition in terms of human personalities.

PSYCHOLOGICAL EFFECTS OF URBANISM

We are indebted to the Protestant theologian J. V. Langmead Casserly for an illuminating analysis of the predominant emotional states in modern urban life.[8] Casserly points to illusion as one of the most significant of these states. The urban person lives in the aura of all those fantasies of social psychology promoted by the vulgar and quasi-erotic advertising of the technical city. The illusions and symbols of politics also find an immense theater for exploitation in the city; propaganda itself has been defined by Harold Lasswell as "the manipulation of significant symbols," more often than not unrelated to reality. Directly related to the vicarious nature of life in a mechanized milieu is the elaborate and bizarre emotional dreaming of modern urbanism.

Class envies, social climbing and frenetic exhibitionism give a tone of irascibility to the emotional climate of the city. The antagonism between racial and ethnic groups and the "total war" fevers of our century express this mass emotional agitation growing out of the nervous irritation of millions. Cities have always had excitable populations; Caesars trembled before the "mobile vulgus" of Rome. The excitation of the modern urban populace, however, is a condition that is subject to great diversity of expression, so that there is a broad area of behavior affected by it in both crude and subtle fashion.

On the other hand, there also exists a tendency toward apathy. The giantism of the metropolis and the inability of the citizen to comprehend events owing to the vicarious quality of his experience and the specialization of labor and social roles, leads him to adopt an indifferent, defeatist or cynical attitude, frequently extending even to his own personal affairs. This apathy results in a tremendous inertia which affects such things as community planning, political participation or civil defense in peacetime. Thus an emotional bias against constructive action is maintained in the face of pressing problems. This attitude is probably exaggerated by the greater proportion of older people in the large city. The natural reserve and caution of the aged probably increases the number of those urbanites who are unable or unwilling to rouse themselves to do justice to the complexity of experience.

The urbanite is often part of the "lonely crowd." Shrinking from a myriad of contacts and stimuli, the urban personality withdraws within itself. There are even flourishing districts in the metropolis based upon the loneliness of citizens; the skid-row, the red-light district, the bohemian area, the bachelor lodgings—all owe something of their existence to loneliness. The conflict of culture in heterogeneous populations produces many persons who fit the description of "the marginal man." The impersonality of life in commercial-industrial centers heightens the paradox of loneliness amid massed populations and intense superficial socialization.[9]

The very size of the populace in major cities makes it possible for the emotional states just mentioned to be grossly exploited. Cults of illusion, irascibility, apathy and loneliness grow up and institutionalize emotionalism. Catharsis and excitation are indulged in for their own sake. Lonely hearts clubs, orgiastic jazz crazes, newspaper "sob" serials and television spectacles bring about the federation of various emotional themes and make these themes publicly powerful. Thus those emotional manifestations which are pathological become regularized into blocs of active sentiment, often at strategic levels of the city. In this fashion such patterns offer a terrifying threat to orderly and humane life. Like Dostoievsky's man from the underground, there are too many urban types who would choose to smash reason and precept and live by whim. John U. Nef has commented upon this tendency: "The conventional idea of the industrial revolution has interposed itself like a dense fog between us and our history. It has contributed to the conceit that the industrialized peoples have emancipated themselves from the irrational and primitive aspects of their nature, instead of having merely changed the character of their aspirations in directions perhaps as irrational as those of their ancestors."[10]

THE SOCIALIZATION OF THE MIND

It has been maintained that the irrational elements in society have come to the fore under modern conditions and that the ideal design, the precedence traditionally accorded reason in Western society, is now overwhelmed by irrationality and confusion.[11] If this is true anywhere, it should be true in the modern metropolis where the spirit of the age is in full reign.

In the modern city with its huge population and speed of communciation, there has occurred what might be called the "socialization of the mind." By this we mean that the individual person has more and more judgments made for him by society. Vast corporations compete in telling the citizen what he ought to think. Affairs of great moment, no less than the minutiae of tonsorial detail, are decided for the citizen. In many instances it could even be proven that the citizen is divested of his rational faculties by the manipulators of common opinion. The activity of the "hidden persuaders" is made continual by the ubiquitous character of mass communications.

Technical society produces in the mind a plethora of complex, symbolic and changing phenomena. It is true that many of these objects are standardized, or superficial in significance, but to the person who must choose, the sheer multiplicity of goods offered by the rich life of urbanism creates a frightful problem of assigning priority and aligning relationships. Abundance, the quality of material goods, and intensity of stimulation put a heavy burden upon the mind. Confronted with gigantic and complex phenomena, it is little wonder that the individual recoils from the task of making independent judgments and relies upon supporting opinions and even superstitions.

The "socialization of the intellect" and the confusion resulting from the welter of objects thrust out for evaluation in the modern city have led some commentators to abandon the rationalist view of man of 18th and 19th century scientism. "What we have learned from the guidance of studies in modern social psychology, with the dismaying spectacle before us of enlarging masses of insecure individuals seeking communal refuge of one sort or another, is that the rationalist image of man is theoretically inadequate and practically intolerable," writes Robert Nisbet.[12] Certainly modern psychology and the historical experience of our time make a strict rationalist interpretation of man impossible. But it is not so much the view which is erroneous as that present conditions do not allow a normal development of the human person. The minds of men are neglected and abused; the intellectual life of man, abortive.

What seems to frustrate rationality and retard thought on the part of masses of men is the lack of the conditions necessary for intellectual efficiency. We have mentioned the emotional stimulation and density of phenomena in the industrial-technical city which tend to take the initiative away from the individual. In the great city, also, time for thought is at a premium. Mass life must be scheduled and coördinated to be bearable, and tight schedules do not wait on thought. Such elementary conditions as silence and stability of life are often simply not present. Hence, the intellect finds its native capacities checked and outstripped. This fact is hidden by the mechanized regulation to which urbanites subscribe. Scheduled events, standardized performances and expectations disguise the underlying intellectual emasculation of the urban masses.

Two notable generalizations can be made about the type of thinking imposed by an urban environment: first, the judgments which occur by the millions in the intense technical milieu are poorly related to one another. We do not mean, of course, that inferences and carefully constructed reasoning are not the rule, but rather that the totality of urban intellectualism is not integrated. A changing and complex environment works with unremitting power against the integration of ideas; generalized synthesis becomes harder, and specialization tyrannizes over all.

The achievements and dangers of specialization have been pointed out with increasing frequency: "Specialization of knowledge and disintegration of man's personality go together. Both have produced results impressive in detail but these results await unification. They have been achieved at the cost of human and social values and of the personal life of man. If we are sincere and courageous, we must admit that we are standing before a gigantic heap of fragments which we cannot put together and restore to their old form."[13]

Secondly, it is characteristic of urban intellectualism that ideas are not valued in themselves. Ideas are means to ends and not expressions of the spirit of man. The life of contemplation is not understood, admired or considered socially acceptable. It is not useful enough. At least, this is the prevailing social outlook. It is often apparent in the way in which the fine arts are neglected in the modern city while huge throngs dote upon cheap pastimes which produce immediate crude pleasure. The emphasis upon material goods and standards in the productive technical societies underlies an intellectual expediency which seeks to enact life with as little thought as possible.

Whether or not there is philosophical agreement on the meaning of the person or on the ultimate significance of man, each individual is faced with the practical problem of making some estimation of the person if only in an egotistical sense. This process is extremely difficult in the great city, where the individual is forced to carry out the process of interpreting his personality without the benefit of continuous intelligible social experience or the assistance of strong canons of group interpretation. Under the pressures of forces which he himself cannot control, uprooted from a former style of life, related to the community chiefly in an economic way, the individual tends to be overwhelmed with his own helplessness and insignificance.

THE NORMLESS ATTITUDE

In such a situation the values which can be derived and adhered to are subjected to extreme pressure. Aside from the emotional and intellectual difficulties which we have already mentioned, the individual is thus confronted with an intense clash of value systems. Margaret Mead has commented upon this conflict of values and the experience to which values must be applied: "American children are growing up in a culture where, for several generations, each generation's experience has differed sharply from the last, and in which the experience of the youngest child in a large family will be extraordinarily different from that of the first born. . . . So long standing and so rapid have been these processes of change that expectation of change and anxiety about change have been built into our character as a people."[14]

Thus for every change there is the necessity of reëvaluation, and the changes are momentous and continual. The clash of value systems, no matter how subjectively these systems may be wrought, is a condition which deeply affects personality formation and the final definition of the human person. In the United States competitiveness and gregariousness, for instance, contend for supremacy as modes of behavior. Scientific skill and vulgarity of taste contrast everywhere. Huge corporate projects requiring great coördination and the most zealous individualist sentiment are set in juxtaposition.

The individual, in order to resolve some of the conflicts presented to him, will often make a unitary allegiance, not to confusing social goals or systems, but to a thing, a tangible process or machine. He surrenders to impersonality in the form of non-human phenomena. More serious and perhaps more frequent, however, is the surrender to indecision as a personal orientation. The urbanite, confused amid cultural conflict and change, adopts a "normless" attitude, trying to remain oblivious of deeper personal or social standards. This results in a frightening ethical ambivalence. Judgment is suspended on any great issue such as God, creation, death, or the meaning of society. And as Berdyaev has written: "Where there is no God, there is no man." The meaning of man becomes arbitrary and clouded. The definition of the person becomes heedlessly disregarded and lesser issues are fretted over endlessly.

If the meaning and essential character of the human person is lacking, then a cultural prerequisite for social organization is lacking and the city is weakened in its cultural mission of serving man. Only a comprehensive, integrated and enduring interpretation of the person can provide the basis for modern urban society.[15]

THE THREAT TO HUMAN FREEDOM

A final point must be made regarding the volitional life of the urban person. Modern depth psychology has challenged many psychological traditions and introduced a fluid and boldly exploratory concept of personality. One of the effects of this new psychology, as well as of the philosophical pragmatism of our day, has been the denial or the obscuring of the reality of the will in human actions. Thus in the dominant formal social thought and in the popular opinion of the urban public, the existence of the will is either denied or regarded as a highly tenuous, semi-fictional idea.

As a consequence, the marketing practices, political appeals and recreation cults of the great city play upon emotional impulse and biological response.[16] Choices are obscured, denied or made meaningless. "Impulse buyers," "habitual voters," and "captive audiences" are the norm. The will is so circumscribed with minute and regularized social restrictions that few significant daily choices are called for.

In addition, the comforts and protections afforded by city life are hardly conducive to the training of the will. Asceticism, at any rate, is not a working ideal, and a headlong pursuit of "higher standards of living" is encouraged on every hand. Pastel-tinted suburbs and sleek air-conditioned offices are not the most auspicious environments in which to encourage self-control and strong will power. The revolutionary city with its economy of abundance, mass communications, diversions and distractions creates an atmosphere where volitional activity is intensively compressed and frustrated.

The revolutionary industrial city is in its essence a city saturated with technology. Even more than the political deliriums which have sown carnage among the nation states, the technology which has so often been the servant of political ferocity is the real threat to freedom and to the human will in the modern world. The dictatorships of the 20th century have not won such a permanent or universal allegiance among men as have the rewards of technology and applied science. The political foes of freedom have found it possible to use technology as the means to their ends of total power, and the masses have repeatedly betrayed the ends of the tyrants without renouncing the technological lures and commitments which have made them so susceptible to tyranny in the first place.

The power of technology to weave a dictatorial way of life even without a political dictator has been proven by the uncritical adherence of the masses to the first fruits of the industrial revolution. The effects and portents of certain inventions and mechanical achievements was not at all clear, but these inventions were enthusiastically received and popularly cherished with eager, almost superstitious, optimism by the industrial proletariat. Mass production fed mass consumption in something resem-

bling a Pavlovian orgy. The technical and material outpouring which exists in the revolutionary city threatens
so to hamper the critical abilities of man that he will become a sort of psychological eunuch, human only up to a
point, and bereft of his ability to make use of his will for
social control—and social survival.[17]

The personalist philosophers have dwelt upon this problem in defiance of ever mounting trends against volunta-
rism. Gabriel Marcel writes:

. . . The real problem is to know to what degree an administrative machine can be informed with spiritual values, and
it is very hard not to feel very pessimistic when dealing with
this problem. There seems to be a chance of a positive solution
only in the case in which what looks from the outside like a
mere administrative machine, in reality conceals a structure of
quite a different sort, founded on values experienced and recognized as such. But the organizational giantism which technocracy seems inevitably to imply excludes precisely these
humanizing conditions . . . unless we make a truly ascetic
effort to master techniques and put them in their proper and
subordinate place, they tend to organize themselves around
the man who rejects.[18]

The cumulative enslavement to the minutiae of technically and mechanically dominated life is hastened by
the atomized social relations of the industrial city. The
person, protected in only a nominal fashion by the Western humanist ideals because of generations of philosophical erosion, presents an isolated target for the onslaughts of
depersonalization. Those jealous of human freedom see in
this situation a potent formula for oppression and coercion: "If we fail to rebuild this City of ours with the

cement of creative spontaneity and love there will always be a tyranny to impose on us from without the unity we have allowed ourselves to lose from within."[19]

Men have for ages come together under the influence of God, or their gods as conceived by them, to conduct their community life. In the modern city men come together under the influence of the machine, in subservience to machines, to conduct the technical life which is intrinsic to the new urbanism. Both the social values and expressions of the religious life of man are too frequently stunted in the technical city. As a consequence, religious commitment often cannot result in either authentic cultural formation or spiritual development, and thus creative interaction between the individual and his community is either repressed or rendered haphazard. Many of the endowments which united and fraternal religious association bring to the personality have been compromised, and hence civic life, which ultimately is based upon the ability of individuals as citizens to support coöperative effort is undermined.

If art is, as Claudel says, "the world clamoring to become one city," then this art has been dissipated. The spirit of communion, reverence, continuity, naturalness and integrity imparted by worship which is communally expressed is lacking in revolutionary urbanism, because these values are not manifest in the personalities produced by urbanism. In the words of Pius XII, "It is as if everything had conspired to make more difficult for men and Christians the preservation of their personal dignity—nay, even to make it impossible."[20] Thus the entire religio-cultural process for the refinement of the social person has weakened, while the civic responsibilities of the city man have been tremendously increased.

NOTES

1. Romano Guardini, *The End of the Modern World* (New York: Sheed and Ward, 1956), pp. 56-57.
2. Richard Neutra, in *Progressive Architecture* (August 1956), p. 98.
3. Rudolph Allers, *The Psychology of Character* (New York: Sheed and Ward, 1953), p. 13.

   R. E. Faris and H. W. Dunham, *Mental Disorders in Urban Areas* (Chicago: University of Chicago Press, 1939).

   Karen Horney, *The Neurotic Personality in our Time* (New York: W. W. Norton Co., 1937).
4. See R. A. Bauer, *The New Man in Soviet Psychology* (Cambridge: Harvard University Press, 1952); José Ortega y Gasset, *The Revolt of the Masses* (New York: W. W. Norton Co., 1932), p. 80; Henri de Lubac, "The New Man—the Marxist and the Christian View" in *Cross Currents* (Fall, 1950).
5. Max Lerner, *America as a Civilization* (New York: Simon and Schuster, 1957), p. 168.
6. See Elton Mayo, *Social Problems of an Industrial Civilization* (Cambridge: Harvard University Press, 1946).
7. For data relating to the decline of physical competence see reports of such studies as those of Dr. R. J. DuBos of the Rockefeller Institute for Medical Research (New York *Times*, May 20, 1958) and Dr. Hans Kraus (New York *Times*, April 24, 1954).
8. J. V. L. Casserly, "The Children of God in the City of Man" in *The Metropolis in Modern Life*, ed. by R. M. Fisher (Garden City: Doubleday and Co., Inc., 1955).
9. David Reisman, *The Lonely Crowd* (New Haven: Yale University Press, 1950); M. M. Wood, *Paths of Loneliness* (New York: Columbia University Press, 1953).

10. John U. Nef, *War and Human Progress* (Cambridge: Harvard University Press, 1950), p. 300.

11. John H. Hallowell, *Main Currents in Modern Political Thought* (New York: Henry Holt Co., 1950); see especially the chapter "The Revolution of Nihilism," p. 521.

12. Robert Nisbet, *The Quest for Community* (New York: Oxford University Press, 1953), p. 229.

13. E. A. Gutkind, *Revolution of Environment* (London: Routledge, Kegan Paul, Ltd., 1957), p. 56.

14. Quoted in *Catholic Charities Review* (December, 1951). For a definition of values see Ralph Linton, *The Cultural Background of Personality* (New York: Appleton-Century-Crofts, Inc., 1945), p. 111.

15. Paul Halmos, *Towards a Measure of Man* (London: Routledge, Kegan, Paul, Ltd., 1957). The author argues that a normal man exists in society and his needs form the basis of a social ethic. He argues almost entirely from researches in sociology, psychology and anthropology, not from philosophical or ethical principles. See also *Solitude and Privacy* by the same author and publisher.

16. See Abraham Low, *Mental Health through Will Training* (Boston: Christopher Publishing House, 1950), pp. 138-140 and T. V. Moore, *Personal Mental Hygiene* (New York: Grune and Stratton, 1945). This well known priest-psychologist interprets mental illness as a deviation from an ideal of perfection. In his opinion mental life is a continuum, and small aberrations can accumulate to overwhelm the personality; hence the need for volitional control in small matters.

17. John U. Nef, *The Cultural Foundations of Industrial Civilization* (Cambridge; Cambridge University Press, 1957), p. 151. "The verification and cultivation of the highest human attributes—charity, love, honor, justice, clear thinking—depend on the human personality, which the scientist and the statistician leave out of account. It is neither in the rise of modern science nor in the rise of modern economics that the cultural foundations of 'civilization' can be mainly found. Their principal sources were the partially successful efforts to practice a Christian life in the temporal world and to bring about an

alliance between the quest for beauty and the quest for virtue, in a society dedicated to delight."

18. Gabriel Marcel, *Man Against Mass Society* (Chicago; Henry Regnery Co., 1952), pp. 153, 195.

19. Gustav Thibon, *Christianity and Freedom* (New York: Philosophical Library, 1956), p. 17.

20. In his address of July 17, 1952.

3. The Urban Family

3

The Urban Family

A THOUGHTFUL man can see the evils of society by look-
ing into the eyes and hearts of his own sons. This is so
because the family necessarily reflects the ways of society. In every society, the family is the prototype and
the check unit of social relations. Without efficiently func-
tioning domestic life there can be no cultural continuity.
Although the immensely resourceful social machinery of
the revolutionary city tends to obscure its role, domestic
life is the vastly influential foundation beneath the elaborate institutional structure of the modern urban center,
controlling the basic human life urges and working as the
matrix of all social systemization. And yet, in the revolutionary city there is perhaps no social institution which is
so consistently undermined, compromised and afflicted by
conditions outside itself.

These conditions are sometimes matters of default. In
an urban environment, the community codes which usually define and reinforce the function of the family are
weak. When contacts between people tend to be anonymous and transitory and there are great variations in
culture to cope with, a kind of confused tolerance is practiced rather than a generally accepted value system.

Other conditions which drastically affect family life are more directly related to an industrial order which has meant congested housing, the separation of the head of the family from the home in the daytime, the employment of women in industry, and the development of social services to substitute for some of the functions formerly performed in the home.

The ways in which the revolutionary city affect family life will become clearer if we pose several inquiries. What are some of the peculiar urban conditions surrounding family life? How well does the family carry out its function of the physical sustenance of life in the modern city? Does the family continue to perform its traditional role as a transmitter of social and cultural values in the city? What attitudes and ideas are influential in forming the pattern of life of the urban family? Answering these questions will not, perhaps, give us a total analysis of the conditions under which the Christian family must perform, but it will permit us to see the relationship of metropolitan life to its major functions.

THE DEPENDENT FAMILY: ECONOMICS

At the basic level of economic function, the family is severely restricted. As economic units, most urban families are reduced to the role of consumers, and even their consumption is carried out under circumscribed conditions. Lacking the security of productive property, the urban family seeks economic protection in the conspicuous consumption of goods and services and in complex systems of insurance or socialized thrift. The actual economic control of urban savings and investments of the latter type seldom rests with the contributing family; it belongs to the corporate combines or government agencies, and the corporate enterprises with which the economic livelihood of urban families is thus intimately connected are not responsive to democratic control to the degree which would permit broad participation in shaping policy. Hence, the urban family is largely a consumer unit in which the consumer decisions are increasingly directed by advertising and the corporation expedients which mass production and distribution dictate. Historically considered, and in terms of real wages, humane surroundings and net worth, modern urban families in privileged areas are probably quite affluent. In terms of economic independence, productive ability and long-range resources, however, the family in the revolutionary city is in an extremely weak economic position.[1]

Families living in cities where exploitive industrialism is practiced (as it was during most of the 19th century in the United States and England) without social conscience or government restraint can expect little but a callous attrition exercised in the name of economics. But even in the world of reformed capitalism, the very complexity of the technical order on which the urban family depends makes it economically vulnerable. This system, as we have noted, has successfully sustained phenomenal population growth and has raised living standards, but it is subject to periodic depressions, and terrible wars have occurred under its regime. The social costs to the family of *laissez faire* capitalism will only be fully known as the family is forced to cope with the challenges of modern times. To cite but one example, the effects upon the family of warfare which is based upon urban productive systems are incalculable, and this warfare is entering the atomic phase wherein millions of families can be annihilated almost instantaneously. The economics of the modern city has conferred abundance on many and made volatile and intricately dependent the sustenance and social functions of the greater proportion of metropolitan families.

Two other effects of the contemporary industrial order are worthy of note: First, the family has been strongly influenced, and in the case of the economically productive elite "captured," by the corporation. The conditions under which the family lives, the training its members receive, the goals to which they aspire and the works which fill their lives are dictated by the corporation. What the clan was to the ancient world and feudalism was in medieval times, the corporation is to the modern era.[2]

Secondly, the economic system which supports the revolutionary city has made acquisitive materialism an overriding ideal of the family life of millions. We might call it "the beloved sickness." Every advancement in material living standards leads to a restless craving for the next; every amenity won, to a passion for another without regard to the utility, economy or wisdom of such a ritual of aggrandizement.

THE EQUIVOCAL FAMILY: VALUES

If we look beyond the economic basis of metropolitan life to the social patterns which make up the setting for family living, we find that a number of highly variable influences work upon the function of the family. Mobility, latitude and lack of integration are the distinctive characteristics of this social setting. Traditional formulations of family living are discarded and a wide variety of family organization and behavior patterns enacted in pragmatic and experimental fashion. Vocational and class groups, ethnic, religious and racial groups, regional variations and popular cults all contribute to a heterogeneity which presents to every family a variety of ways of domestic life. Despite the increased physical standardization of such things as housing, entertainment and civic services, this diversity of ideology and practice in family life continues.

The variegated family patterns in the metropolis have evoked what might be called the dominant type of American family. Unable to choose from all of the free-ranging, polyglot and popularized versions of family life some one definitive system around which to build a tradition, urban dwellers have made flexibility, adaptation and eclectic trial their approach. Although the traditionalist patriarchal family is still with us, and economic and minority influences still create differences, an archtypal urban and suburban family ideal can be discerned. This family is produced by physical mobility, technical surroundings, a "sex revolution" (as Pitirim Sorokin calls it) and a dissolution of paternal domestic authority. It is a family which prides itself on its internal egalitarianism, its quasi-hedonism, its child pampering and its ability to rove freely among a potpourri of familial arrangements without subscribing to any but the most accidental standards.

Sociologists, who are fond of assigning names to such phenomena, may in time specify this ascendant urban family type as the "equivocal" or the "arbitrary" family. The mobility, emotionalism and ersatz cosmopolitanism forced on the urban family by mass media and rapid transportation make it extremely difficult for these families to define their standards and the roles of their members within the home and in community life.*

FAMILY LIVING: HOUSING

This problem is exaggerated by the failure of modern cities to produce an integrated and vigorous local community life. This is apparently one of the prices we have paid for technological and industrial success. Historically, the local community has represented the vital synthesis between physical environment and cultural achievement. This has not been true in the revolutionary city, where local life tends to be vestigial, based on ethnic remainders or heedless convenience. It is even hard to find professional planners who will seriously concede its existence.

The central factor in local community life is housing, the sheltering of families. The inability of the mass urban

---

* The talented and creative elite who reap the rewards of urbanism to the fullest extent are only a little more successful in attaining stability than the bourgeois and underprivileged families. The nominal head of such a family is at a grave disadvantage in measuring his community responsibilities. He is described by one writer ". . . as having no roots in the city. It is debatable at least whether he will ever put down roots in his 'exurb', but certainly he had none in New York. And he was bound to feel this more keenly, working as he was in a profession which is itself so rootless, so insecure, so transitory." A. C. Spectorsky, *The Exurbanites* (New York: J. P. Lippincott, 1955), p. 262

society to provide good housing in humane and tolerable surroundings has been one of the major reasons for the abandonment of local life. This fact and the influence of technological forces which transcend and overbear the residential locality have submerged the neighborhood in a welter of traffic, bad and mediocre housing, and commercial giantism.

The quality of housing itself must be related to the physical setting around it. As industrialism grew, families by the millions were domiciled according to a distorted economic utility near mills and factories, harbors and railroads. Even the homes free of these ugly surroundings were set out in rigid mechanical blocks which had only the most crude relation to the needs of families and the features of the natural landscape. The fiercely persistent center-city slums, the circling shanty towns and the immigrant and Negro ghettoes "across the tracks" became a permanent, and in many cases a dominant, housing arrangement in great cities. The building booms of the revolutionary city in its advanced stages have been explosions which proliferated in a random, ill-conceived and erratic fashion.

The suburban expansion of the metropolis has reduced the oppression of the industrial environment and performed a symbolic gesture toward natural surroundings, but it has done so at the cost of standardization and a great degree of government control of the housing industry. With this prospect, it is little wonder that Patrick Geddes remarked that modern housing increasingly consisted of "slums, semi-slums, and super-slums."

According to census estimates, only about two-thirds

of our housing is passable by the most simple measurements.[3] In many cities high land costs have led to the building of high-density elevator apartment buildings to replace deteriorated tenements and slum blocks. These structures are at best poorly suited to family living, and often seem to be actual agents of family and community disorganization. "Nowhere is it quite so difficult to create a community as in a block of flats," writes a British expert.[4] Despite these shortcomings, current housing concepts do promise some relief after a century of jerry building, hand-me-down and wasteful conversion. The sway of fad and fashion may at last be restricted by gradual rediscovery of planning and architecture as humane disciplines.

But this promise of good housing in abundance through an architecture freed from industrial vassalage and through a prudent use of technology is threatened by the cultural confusion which plagues the architecture of home building. One of America's mass builders, William Levitt (who has been shortsighted enough to name his constructions after himself), has stated that in the home-buying process "a purchaser . . . is not just buying a house, he's buying a way of life." The vast construction of American housing is largely a sham-built panorama of the planning ineptitude and aesthetic immaturity which afflict our way of life. "The American's home was never his castle," writes one British critic, "it does not even afford him privacy. . . . The kitchen is little more than a place for storing and warming food. . . . The living room has been turned into the meanest sort of auditorium, unfit for conviviality, and probably no other civilization has produced gardens as melancholy as ours. . . . But these shortcomings are either not recognized or they are taken for granted as part of our cultural pattern."[5] Hence, in one city after another the erratic urban residential sprawl is repeated: a core of decrepit, exploited and abused structures, a belt of monotonous, ill-planned workingmen's units, and then a scattering of speculative miscellany leading on out into suburbia.

The disparate housing pattern of the modern city physically prevents a clear focus of domestic and recreational life. Mobility and mass entertainment distract families from the local scene. Thus the urbanite leaps from the springboard of the home directly into the mainstream of metropolitan life. There is no intervening communal structure to organize opinion, refine desires, develop responsibility and provide an organic community framework for reference in urban affairs. This lack of a local community order is the source of both familial and civic weakness in the great city. Unless a community structure can be created for our new urbanism, the family will continue to be prey to the powerful forces which can so easily frustrate and distort it. What is needed is ". . . a sense and quality of neighborhood order, an order thoroughly related to the need for regaining family scale, one in which the mass housing concept of endless repeats of today's 'projects' are broken down to size . . . one in which the engineers' concept of cost value will be judged always against the enduring qualities of family needs and relationships."[6]

If a concept of community life can be composed around the domestic sphere, with housing conditions as the central concern, then the other community facilities—commercial, cultural and recreational—can be placed in relation to domestic needs, free of the overwhelming domination of industrial enterprises.

IDEOLOGIES: INDIVIDUALISM, MATERIALISM AND HUMANITARIANISM

Having considered some of the physical and economic conditions surrounding the family in the technological city, let us move on to a very brief view of some of the outstanding ideological influences shaping family life. It has already been noted that formal ideologies of family life are not held by most American families; often the family is only an institution in a symbolic sense. Nevertheless, the whole of its life is geared to certain assumptions.

In the first place, the intensive individualism propagated by city life has reduced the family to a network of relationships devoted to the service of individual happiness. This individualism is as much a product of physical conditioning as it is a strong echo of the 19th century philosophers. It stems in part, for example, from the fact that migration to the city has been primarily a migration of single persons who have had to face the city alone. Whatever its source, individualism is the staple of urban relationships and is anterior, as it were, to family life. Operating as a solvent, it denudes the family of institutional features and weakens the domestic allegiance of parents, children and other kin alike.

Second, a kind of parody of a system of beliefs could be constructed by substituting material values for social or spiritual ones; the goals of reproduction, education, mutual assistance and well-being have their absurd counterparts in materialist facts of life. Reproduction of material gadgets, education for economic action and mutual exchange of goods and comforts would be the operative principles of domestic life in the system. Economic hedonism, the "beloved sickness," is a potent force molding urban thinking on family life.

A vague humanitarianism is a third current of thought which permeates urban family life. The effect of this humanitarian outlook has been to mitigate the more obvious anti-domestic conditions in urban life such as child-labor, widespread prostitution and parental cruelty, but the simplist and sentimentalist attitudes implicit in popular humanitarianism have been incapable of grappling with the real sources of family weakness. It is one of the causes of child-centered or-dominated communities about which one writer has remarked: "Consider a moment how middle-class people reason. They have such a high standard of the preciousness of children, the care they are entitled to, the room they need, the education they must get, that they don't have the children at all, or they have 1.8. Must we not somewhat consider this reasoning as a rationalization of a wish not to be bothered, a fear of risking?"[7] And middle-class views are the cultural hallmarks of our urban populace.

The three social attitudes mentioned above combine with the economic and community conditions of the metropolis to bring great pressure on the family. Not only are rigid or trustee systems of familism shattered under the strain, but families in which a moderate degree of authority is attempted tend to lose their identity as families. This failure to maintain the integrity of the family has led Carl Zimmerman to assign the term "nihilism" to our attitudes toward family. "The very continuation of our culture seems to be inextricably bound up with this nihilism in family behavior. That the family of the immediate future will move further toward atomism seems highly probable."[8] Is the severity of this judgment warranted? If we examine just how well the family performs its basic functions in the revolutionary city, we will be better able to answer this question.

A number of sociologists have long held that no large city reproduces itself. They argue that the technical industrial city of more than 100,000 population usually discourages marriage by about 10 per cent, that the percentage of single, widowed and divorced are higher at all age levels in the city than in rural areas, and that children are clearly an economic liability, especially in view of meager housing accommodations, so that contraception is a common practice. On the other hand, infant mortality is still being decreased, and the populations of cities have made remarkable gains in health and life expectancy.

Whether the metropolis can sustain population that is stable and not subject to diminution in its reproductive functions probably cannot be answered because we lack adequate knowledge of the relationships between the new rationalized ruralism and the advanced form of increasingly suburbanized metropolis. Will the metropolis continue to depend, as it has, on immigration to make up its population deficiencies? There is evidence to indicate that rural migration to cities will diminish rapidly in the United States in the next decade. Nor do we know enough about the effect of economics upon reproduction and population growth. It does seem clear that the metropolis as it has existed, especially the "core" city, has offered radical discouragement to reproduction. The drain of hyperstimulating big-city life upon the nervous system and the effects of what Lewis Mumford calls "vicarious vitality" through diversion upon reproduction are not understood. If the city is to afford favorable conditions for fuller family life and population maintenance, then the city must change greatly in economics, social habits and community development. The steady population rise in the United States from 1940 to 1960, despite the fact that the nation is increasingly urbanized, would suggest that perhaps the conditions of big-city life have been tempered sufficiently, especially by suburbia, so that there is at least a population equilibrium in the urban centers augmented by cityward migration.[9]

THE CULTURAL MISSION OF THE FAMILY

Even if we conjecture that the modern city can reproduce itself and sustain a biologically productive family life, this only partly illuminates the question of how family life fares in our new environment. If we are to have a developing social life, then our families must engage in: ". . . a process whereby a full realization or fulfillment of human capacities is gradually attained . . . that society might be regarded as most developed which evokes the most devotion to common ends among its members and releases the greatest fund of intelligent energy. . . . It is clear that ethical and biological criteria cannot be assumed to coincide without careful examination. . . ."[10]

Cultural formation, or education in the broadest sense, is the area in which the ravages of the urban forces of disorganization are most clearly evident. The instability of the urban family frequently does not permit the consistent working out of a system of cultural norms for children. The training for personal and social life which should be conferred in the basic social unit of the family is confused by unclear lines of authority, the intervention of the stereotyped stupidity of the mass media and widespread but disguised ignorance of parental obligations. Absurd courtship patterns, cultural conflicts, the cult of unrealistic romance and the lack of family traditions explain the great numbers of formal breakdowns of families and the uncounted hidden failures which add to the pathology in our cities. Juvenile crime, alcoholism and severe discontent attend this family collapse. The absence of family unity, either physical or intellectual, exaggerates all of these conditions and imperils mental health. Many psychiatrists attribute the great rise in the number of mentally ill to the strains which urbanization has visited upon families.[11]

In the urban setting for home life we have lost the intelligible symbols and social creeds which explain the meaning of domestic existence to each new generation. We have substituted for this system cheap parodies of marital functions which range from whimsical nonsense to sensationalized tragedy. Hence, our misgivings about the ability of urban families to assure biological continuity are succeeded by more conclusive judgments about the family's ability to provide cultural continuity. The seriousness of this failing can hardly be overemphasized. No institution other than the family has the universality, intimacy and adaptive power to transmit the heritage of society. Each family which fails in its fundamental social mission brings the specter of social collapse one step closer.

It should be pointed out that our urban families have increased their activities in superficial directions while neglecting their basic responsibilities. In response to the complexity and giantism of the metropolis, the family has tried to extend its functions to embrace the multitude of transient contacts big-city life entails. In doing so, it has failed because of the sheer scale of urban diversity to perform the basic tasks of the supervision and guidance of family members.[12] The civilizing influence of strong family life has, in turn, been curtailed, so that suburban ennui and mediocrity, the individualist frigidity of mass apartment living and the "problem family" chaos of government housing projects and slums occupy a growing portion of the urban scene in place of stable and resilient domestic life.

A part of this failure, perhaps, is related to the estrangement of the urban family from nature. In the modern urban world, man has lost contact with natural things, and this lack is one of the conditions responsible for his cult of acquisition. Unable to establish relationships based upon an organic adjustment to nature, the modern family, and the millions who have cut themselves off from familism, lose some of the central values of human tradition which support domestic and civic life. This being the

case, the folk life of the metropolitan urbanite becomes
mechanized, and on occasion morbid—the "pavement culture" which is decried by so many critics of urbanism.[13]

The problem is not exclusively an American one.
Throughout the world the spread of urbanism has imposed a crisis upon the attempts of families to perform
their elemental function of transmitting values. The influences of mass secular school systems, mass communications, mobility, anti-family philosophies and popular
nihilism have ridden roughshod over the efforts of the
urban family to transmit coherent social and spiritual
values. Countries as diverse as Puerto Rico and Ireland,
Brazil and China are experiencing this process.[14] The
urban family exists everywhere in what is claimed to be a
value-free atmosphere. What is meant is the general skepticism about values in the face of so many conflicting
ideals. ". . . An increasing number of people come to the
point where they 'don't know what to think.' Out of this
arises a shifting of the bases of value systems themselves
—from social to individual. More and more the individual
sees only his immediate interest, because the social and
long term individual values are difficult for him to vis-
ualize."[15]

In this chapter we have tried to review the social conditions surrounding family life in great cities and to examine the performance of families under these conditions.
It seems evident from this examination that the functional
prerequisites for wholesome and stable family life are
lacking in the greater proportion of industrialized urban
areas. The group life of the basic social unit is beset with
extreme difficulties. The reproductive function is perhaps

curtailed; the natural basis of physical and social life is distorted; and the family in the new urban areas is usually in a position of economic dependence. These circumstances have undercut the cultural integrity and influence of family life.

The familism of the Western Christian tradition has been gradually subverted till it hardly resembles that domestic ideal which served as a basis for coöperative civic federation in the cities of the West in former ages. In our time it seems quixotic to recall the dicta which related family and city in the institutional sense, such as the formula of St. Thomas Aquinas that, "the fact that a man forms part of a family causes him to form part of a city, which is composed of many families." The institutional framework of city life is not familial but industrial, commercial and individualist. Yet, within this framework the irreducible vital movement of domestic life still imparts a surprising social force to our urban centers. If one concedes that residential considerations exert an increasing influence on cities as the exploitive capitalist system mellows, it can be argued that the family is actually determining the shape of urban areas. As Christopher Tunnard says, "The movement to the outskirts, the whole decentralizing tendency of the contemporary city, is not a movement of individuals, bankers or factory workers, it is a movement of families."[16]

The whole suburban trend may represent an action of social mobility on the part of millions of American families, but another observer does not see in it an expression of new family values, or indeed, of anything but another cycle of massed individualist discontent:

The writer's own feeling is that until there is a definite movement of people out of the metropolitan districts, or until the suburban districts are rather completely reorganized to make a satisfactory home and community life possible to all their residents, we cannot properly consider the suburban movement as accomplishing the purpose aimed at in decentralization. The movement of a considerable number of people from the central cities to the suburbs as they are now organized, or shall I say in their present unorganized condition, does not seem to me to be accompanied by any very significant change in manner of life. It represents merely an individual flight from less to more tolerable surroundings, and it is certainly symptomatic of a revolt against the constraints of congested living, but it involves no clear break with the established values of city living. At the most, therefore, it is only beginning to prepare a population for the establishment of a new social structure in which the values associated with home and children, community life and friends, and living and cooperating with nature will have a better chance to develop than in our cities. Just because it is an unorganized movement of individuals, it can do little more than prepare for the reception of new values; it is no guarantee of their development.[17]

There are some who contend that the social disruption experienced by families in the modern city is not only inevitable, but necessary for the drastic transformation required to break with the ruralism of previous history.[18] But the disorganization of broken families, mass insecurity and overcrowding would seem poor forerunners of a successful new way of life.

A SPIRITUAL VOID

The responses of organized religion to the disorganization threatening family life have been uneven and un-

equal to the magnitude of these innovations. The rural or immigrant religious backgrounds of the vast numbers of families which have been plunged into the new technical metropolis have not yet been adapted to strongly confront the unparalleled strains upon family life. Courtship, sex mores, marriage customs and legislation, portrayals of marriage and the roles and authority of marriage partners have become secularized. The defense by religious groups is too often undertaken without reference to the conditions of labor and community life which so gravely influence the domestic sphere. How often have we heard vapid generalizations and platitudes proferred as counsel to families who are being slowly strangled spiritually by the staccato efficiency of anti-family organizations operating the economics and communications of big cities.

Protestant denominations have probably fared worse than Catholicism in the struggle to maintain the sanctity and integrity of family life in the metropolis. Strong individualism and a tendency toward permissiveness, ambiguity and majority rule in doctrinal matters have hampered Protestant family-life work. The predominantly rural experience of American Protestantism has also constituted a disadvantage for denominations suddenly immersed in urban problems.

Catholicism has had a long, direct relationship with great segments of the urban immigrant population and a clearly expressed, comprehensive and bold program for the "reconstruction of the social order."[19] This program has produced a creative array of experiments such as the priest workers, secular institutes of lay workers, housing coöperatives, and family assistance programs. Parts of it have been adopted by the Christian Democratic parties of Europe. The campaign for social reconstruction has also had the constant leadership and encouragement of the Papacy. On the subject of housing, for example, the Popes have often spoken, always relating their remarks to the spiritual welfare of families.[20] Such spokesmen as Abbé Pierre, the priest who drew the attention of the world to the degrading housing conditions of Paris, have called for urban reform with a fierce zeal. "We must go on shouting it over and over again. We must write it on all the walls and all the public monuments of our towns. The beauty of a town and the beauty of a nation does not lie in museums and theaters and public gardens, nor even in cathedrals. The beauty of a town, in the sight of God and of men, lies in not having slums and homeless people."[21]

Nevertheless, this concerted action has not produced evidence that agencies of religious formation have regained the initiative in urban affairs generally, or in family life in particular, even in the industrial cities where Christianity seems best equipped to conduct its apostolate. This seems particularly true in the United States where the European approaches just mentioned have not inspired any strong American parallel. American Catholics have not been forced by domestic communism, economic deprivation or the tragic damages of war to discover the need for new departures in dealing with social affairs. As a result the Christian family is straitened and pressed into a defensive position.

The family, that "unique cell of the people" as Pope Pius XII called it, remains the social orphan of the revolutionary city. Its vital functions vitiated, deprived of institutional protection and subject to fitful changes of values, the family strives to match the pace of its life against the machine-driven surges of urbanism.

NOTES

1. Even so shrewd a critic of modern capitalism as J. M. Clark seems blandly indifferent to the economic status of the family. See his *Economic Institutions and Human Welfare* (New York: A. Knopf & Co., 1957).
2. William H. Whyte, *The Organization Man* (New York: Doubleday & Co., 1957).
3. Glenn H. Beyer, *Housing—A Factual Analysis* (New York: Macmillan Co., 1958), p. 41.
4. L. E. White, *Community or Chaos: Housing Estates and Their Social Problems,* (London: National Service Council, 1950). See also *Progressive Architecture,* May, 1952, for a keen analysis and criticism of supertenements.
5. Bernard Rudofsky, *Behind the Picture Window* (Oxford University Press, 1955), pp. 7 and 8. See also the Proceedings of the 1957 meeting of the American Institute of Architects: "The speculative builder's house, nine times out of ten, is designed in a pot-pourri of styles whose over-all result is the limitations of the past and the confusion of the present." Architect Leon Chatelain in the *New York Times,* May 15, 1957.
6. Ralph Walker, "The Architect in the Post-War World," *Journal of the American Institute of Architects* (May, 1946).
7. Paul Goodman, *Communitas* (Chicago: University of Chicago Press, 1947).
8. Carl Zimmerman, *The Family and Civilization* (New York: Harper and Brothers, 1947), pp. 797 and 806.
9. Donald Bogue, "Urbanism in the U.S.," in *The American Journal of Sociology* (March, 1955) and C. F. Westoff, "Differential Fertility in the U. S.—1900-1952" in the *American Sociological Review,* 1954. It is interesting to note in this con-

nection that the birth rate for the U.S. Catholic population does not exceed that of the general population except in the upper classes. Rev. Joseph Fichter, S.J., attributes this fact to the urbanization of Catholics. See *America*, February 4, 1950.

10. Morris Ginsberg, *Reason and Unreason in Society* (Cambridge, Harvard University Press, 1948), pp. 32-33.

11. See New York *Times* (March 12, 1957), "Study Links City to Mind's Health". Interesting comment on this topic is available in the 1957 Report of the President of the American Psychiatric Association to the National Health Forum.

12. Robert Nisbet, *The Quest for Community, loc. cit.*, p. 54. "Family, local community, church and the whole network of informal interpersonal relationships have ceased to play a determined role in our institutional system of mutual welfare, education, recreation and economic production and distribution. Yet, despite the loss of these manifest institutional functions, we continue to expect them to perform adequately the implicit psychological or symbolic functions in the life of the individual."

13. B. A. Botkin, *Sidewalks of America* (New York: Bobbs, Merrill Co., 1954). A reading of this compendium of American urban folklore will hardly uncover a single significant cultural custom or item reflecting a religious orientation.

14. See remarks by Rev. I. Illich in New York *Times* (April 8, 1958), as well as "Evolving Irishmen" in *Social Order* (February 1954); F. L. K. Hsu, "The Family in China," in *The Family*, edited by R. N. Anshen (New York: Harper and Brothers, 1949); Marvin Harris, *Town and Country in Brazil* (New York: Columbia University Press, 1956).

15. Carl Zimmerman, *The Family of Tomorrow* (New York: Harper and Brothers, 1949), p. 12.

16. Christopher Tunnard, *The City of Man* (New York: Scribner's Co., 1953), p. 7.

17. Warren S. Thompson, *Cities are Abnormal* (Oklahoma: University of Oklahoma Press n.d.), p. 64. See also *The Exploding Metropolis* by the editors of *Fortune Magazine* (New York: Doubleday Co., 1958).

18. Robert Moses, Construction Coördinator of the City of New York, frequently reflects such a point of view in his zeal for

mammoth projects. For a statement of a tolerant point of view toward urban confusion see Martin Meyerson and B. Terrett, "Metropolis Lost, Metropolis Regained" in the *Annals of the American Academy of Political and Social Science* (November, 1954).

19. See "On the Reconstruction of the Social Order," "On Christian Marriage" and "The Christian Education of Youth," pamphlets published by the America Press, New York.

20. See the messages of Pope Pius XII: Christmas, 1952; *Stations de plein air,* May 3, 1957.

21. *Abbé Pierre Speaks* (New York: Sheed and Ward, 1956), p. 88.

4. The City of God and the Cities of Man

The Protestant Experience
The Catholic Experience
The Parish Community
The Responsibility of the Laity
The Mystical Body

4

The City of God and the Cities of Man

No CITY can be truly conquered unless its altars are conquered. The history of the city teaches us that civic order and fidelity have been constantly associated with religious practice and ideology. This is particularly true of the city life of Western nations where the process of urban organization and development was thoroughly informed by Christian influence. Beneath the mother city of antiquity, Rome of the Empire, bands of early Christians prayed in secret to their risen God, but in time the deities of the ancient world yielded before the exuberance and love of the followers of Christ. From that time until the modern age the cities of the West have been intimately connected with the Christian community; the heroes of the Christians, the saints, have founded cities, defended cities, reformed cities, ransomed cities, and, as their Master before them, wept over cities. The revolutionary city has sown confusion among Christians; the modern industrial metropolis has disrupted the traditional life pattern of the Christians and has opposed a spirit of vanity and aggression to the gospel of humility and Providence.

The astonishing technical advances of Western man

have enabled him to dispense with the religious rationale and usage which are the traditional basis of his community life. By so doing, Western man places himself in an exceptional position, since anthropologists and students have long pointed out that, in T. S. Eliot's lines,

"There is no life that is not in community,
And no community not lived in praise of God."[1]

This concept of community as a link between social organization and a specific locality has permeated Western life. In the Orient social organization is based more upon caste or kinship than upon the free establishment of community ties, but in the West the religious influence of Christianity has fostered and enhanced this freedom of men to exercise his lordship over nature in actual territorial terms.[2]

Since the days of its inception in the hill towns of Galilee, the Christian gospel of love in relationship to God and neighbor has thus exercised its moral leadership and solicitude in civic affairs. The first great Christian classic to follow the Scriptures, St. Augustine's *The City of God,* cast the entire struggle for human salvation in a panoramic analogy of city affairs and events. It was Augustine's admonition that "the city of the ungodly, which did not offer sacrifice to Him alone. . . . could not give to the soul its proper command over the body, nor to the reason its just authority." The high Christian ideals of civic service and social morality implied in this admonition have, in modern Western civilization, been gradually repudiated in favor of philosophical substitutes or simple neopaganism. The effects of this ideological dismemberment upon urban life, particularly in a time of sweeping technical and population changes, have been momentous.

Thus, the modern city, unlike those of the past, is constructed and animated by influences which give it, not a neutral character with respect to religion, but an actively anti-religious spirit. The elements necessary for religious life, such as personal responsibility, standards of asceticism, opportunity for meditation and reliable formulas for conduct, are now opposed by hedonistic economics, powerful distractions and a normless impersonality in social life.

These moral and religious consequences are frequently hidden, however, by the romanticism and glamor of city life. The urbanization of the masses has been accompanied by the growth of mass communication systems which propagate an image that is both mesmerizing and profoundly misleading. The image of the city, particularly that of the American city, is presented to the immigrant or displaced provincial as one of display, affluence, excitement and comfort. Beneath this glamorous idyll-image is the real city of slums, social confusion and disorganization. In this chapter we will look behind the façade of technical urbanism to examine the religious life of Christions in the new environment.

THE PROTESTANT EXPERIENCE

Although this chapter relates primarily to the Catholic tradition, it is necessary to view, however briefly, the reactions of non-Catholic Christianity to the new urbanism. The dissident and Protestant communions which arose

with modern urbanism can be looked to for some indica-
tions of how a highly diversified religious approach fared
in the centuries of vast urbanization. The contrast between the Protestant experience and that of the culturally
integrated and traditionalist Catholic system might thus
contribute to our study of the "captive Christian."

The works of Max Weber and R. H. Tawney propose a
close relationship between Protestant theology and the
rise of that middle-class leadership which promoted urbanization through commercial expansion. Certainly in
the United States the major development of the city took
place under Protestant leadership. Despite this fact, the
pace and dimensions of urbanization very early outstripped the ideological and institutional resources of
Protestantism. The religious diversity within Protestantism and the religiously diverse immigration of the 19th
century overwhelmed the Protestant initiative; as the social strength of Protestantism retreated to the social re-
doubt of the rural areas, the denominations and sects of
the city declined in influence and numbers. H. Paul Douglass found in his studies that by the third decade of this
century an institutional feebleness, impermanence and
high mortality rate afflicted the Protestant churches in
urban areas.[3] There does not seem to have been a reversal
of this process.

Notwithstanding its great flexibility and the religious
initiative which it possessed during the period of American urban expansion, Protestantism has not been able to
confront city conditions with any cohesive mobilization or
stable institutional development of its social resources.
The 19th century episodes of social reform which have

been called the "Protestant Crusade" were largely agrarian in outlook and culminated in the fervor of temperance which ushered in the national prohibition of alcoholic beverages. The role played by Protestantism in fostering political reform in the great cities at the beginning of the present century was certainly notable. The moral indignation produced during this era, however, was the result of sensationalist "muck-raking" journalism and pragmatic civic discontent as well as spontaneous religious leadership. The religious concern for civic morals did not persist in any effective form, lending substance to the cynical opinion that reforms come and go, but political machines endure.

Protestant commentators affirm that their denominations were increasing numerically at mid-century, but many of these commentators express misgivings about the vitality of Protestantism on the urban scene.[4] The increased religious affiliations of urban and suburban Americans may be a genuine beginning of long-term religious growth and effectiveness, or it may merely be the by-product of the urban propensity for developing secondary and transitory associations. Within Protestantism this increase must find its expression in an awareness of complex urban conditions and a coördinated approach to these conditions if numbers are to exert influence. There has been an encouraging growth of concern, research and activity in this direction by the social action departments of the various denominations and in such programs as that of the "group ministry" protagonists in cities like New York. *The City Church*, a publication of the National Council of Churches, has led the way in educating Protestant opinion about urban trends and experiments, and works like Gilbert Beaver's *Christ and Community* ardently champion the potential of Protestantism for the development of social solidarity.[5]

Reinhold Niebuhr has written:

It is interesting that Americans are a more urban people than Europeans. . . . It is also interesting that this urbanness has increased, rather than diminished, loyalty to the religious communities, though it was previously assumed that religious faith flourished on the countryside and withered in the sophisticated air of the city. This did not prove to be so in America. The reason was probably that religious faith in more ways than one was used as an antidote to the simple meanings and fulfillments of a technical culture.[6]

These assumptions would not be conceded by such Protestant leaders as Bernard Iddings Bell. In his trenchant criticism of the moral posture of American society, Bell writes that in cities:

Mores . . . are built up mechanically and anonymously. . . . We still more or less obey statutory law; we pay little heed to unwritten customs of human dignity, or even decency. This is now true not only of such monstrosities as New York or Chicago or Detroit or Los Angeles or of Huston, but of much smaller places. Thanks to frequent migration of vast segments of our people, our cities have ceased to civilize, have ceased to be communities.[7]

This re-evaluation of both doctrine and social affairs now taking place in Protestantism offers promise of a freshened outlook on urban problems. Moreover, coöperation and merger are consolidating various sects and denominations, and a growth in Christain unity will, one hopes, manifest itself in greater social concern over urban problems and build upon the beginnings referred to above.*

THE CATHOLIC EXPERIENCE

The responses of non-Catholic confessions to the revolutionary city must eventually appear less significant than the response of Catholicism. The Roman Catholic Church is a spiritual brotherhood and a social institution with an immense cultural experience and tradition. It is

* The impact of American urban life on Judaism has been such as to break up the ties of communal unity which defied a host of powerful antagonists in European history. "Without community . . . death," says the Talmud. Yet, the family and the synagogue congregation among Jews have been subject to the same weakening as the institutions of other religions.

Since World War II, however, there has been a marked revival of Jewish institutional life. The older immigrant "causes" of socialism, Yiddish culture and the anomalous "secular" Jews have lost stature, and the upholders of ritual and religious viewpoints have been most influential in the religious organization of suburban Judaism and the younger middle-class families. There is no real way of knowing whether the Jew who has cast off the immigrant background and built a temple highly active in community services, but sparse in religious observances, has intensified the religious life of American Jews.

It seems that Jewish groups have not projected any rationale of civic organization which can serve as a platform for urban community restoration. Jews are still so numerically small a group that their religious forms are of limited significance in American life, despite the contributions which Jews make to urban life individually and through their organizations. Cf. Will Herberg, *Protestant, Catholic, Jew* (New York: Harper & Brothers, 1955); and Nathan Glaser, "Judaism in Suburbia, A Sociologist's View," *The Anti-Defamation League Bulletin*, September, 1957.

the largest and most highly organized single religious
body in North America, and the social strength which it
represents has hardly begun to function in any concerted
fashion. In addition it must be emphasized that Catholics
are more than 80 per cent urban dwellers, so that there is
a thoroughgoing connection between urban society and
the role of Catholicism in American national life. The
schools and facilities, the press and opinion which operate
under Catholic auspices are playing an increasing role in
American social affairs. From a minority group, Catholics
are emerging into a full cultural sub-system, large and
active enough to become a decisive factor in the shaping
of social policy and community life, and nowhere is this
more true than on the urban scene.

The local unit of organization of the Catholic Church
is the parish, and it is here that the Catholic Church community is most visible and public. It is through the parish
that the Church is in contact with the family and the local
community. In its sacramental and social functions, the
parish is the direct descendent of the primitive Christian
community which gradually acquired social initiative in
Corinth and Antioch, Alexandria and Rome. From the
sixth century on, the record of parochial definition is
linked with the canonical obligations of the pastor, and
canon law is quite clear and consistent on the commitment of the Church to the parish.[8] Monasticism, missionary extension, war and social upheaval have not altered
this will of the Church to make tangible in local societies
the Kingdom of Christ.

The canonical definition of the parish reached its modern climax in 1918 with publication of the current authori-

tative Code of Canon Law. In the face of the massive dislocations accompanying industrial urban development, the largest church of Christendom affirmed her fidelity to the territorial parish. This assertion of the Catholic ecclesiastical tradition must be viewed in relation to the sociological realities which surround modern American urban Christianity if we are to understand the dilemma of Christians in the revolutionary city. We must see the Catholic parish in a social situation which has shifted cultural life beyond the control of the organized religions.

Although the American Catholic parish has developed in a dynamic environment, several social realities did persist amid the changes. These realities continue to influence the parochial system. First, the American parish is almost invariably a rather new foundation; the number of parishes more than a century old is relatively small. This has meant that, as new institutions, the parishes have often been feeble, particularly in terms of their ability to see beyond the immediate problems of physical construction and organization. The amount of innovation and sacrifice involved in setting up thousands of new parishes has been tremendous. Moreover, a number of grave difficulties, such as the dissensions about trusteeism, plagued the infant Church in one city after another in the 19th century. These disputes have left a legacy of uneasiness which still affects relations between the clergy and the laity.

Second, American parishes have been influenced by the phenomenal immigration which has made our social history unique. Immigrant groups in the major cities set up their "language" and "nationality" parishes and adorned them with the customs and orientation of their former countries. During the 19th century immigrants were encouraged to stay in the cities of the East where priests were available to minister to them. This fact along with the poverty and ethnic cohesion of the immigrants helps account for the massing of the Catholic population in the East. The difficulty of immigrant adjustment and the educational level of the immigrant threw the burden of leadership upon the clergy, where it has remained. The problem of developing a broad base of competent lay leadership is still with the Church in the United States.

The response of the Catholic immigrant to the burgeoning technical city life was neither planned nor comprehensive. In most cases it was unsophisticated and compliant. The formation of ethnic ghettoes was a cultural "reflex action" of self-preservation, and the ethnic parishes produced Catholics with a retiring, ghetto mentality rather than a missionary outlook upon American society. There was, perhaps, an inevitability in this response of the Catholic immigrant to the new conditions, but it has deeply influenced our urban parish life.

The one group to adopt a partially aggressive attitude toward the city were the Catholic Irish immigrants. Lacking a language barrier, and fed by a long-term immigration, the Irish took avidly to politics and the growing ecclesiastical structure. But even here the extent of the urban changes was not realized, and the Irish view of the city was likely to be one merely of wry skepticism, as in the following comment written for the waggish Mr. Dooley by P. F. Dunne: "I've been up to the top iv the very highest buildin' in town, Hinnissey, an' I wasn't anny nearer Hivin thin if I was in the sthreet. The stars was as far away as iver. An down beneath is a lot of us runnin' an' leppin' an' jumpin' about, pushin' each other over, haulin' little sthrips iv iron to pile up in little buildin's called skyscrapers—but not be the sky: workin' day an' night to make a masheen that'll carry us from one jack rabbit colony to another an' yellin' 'Pro-gress! Pro'gress! Ohoo!' Don't they think they're playin' hell. . . ." Novels like *The Cardinal*, by C. M. Robinson, and *The Last Hurrah*, by Edwin O'Connor, depict the Irish Catholic involvement in big city affairs.

Lastly, except for the Spanish missions in the Southwest, the parishes were founded in heterogeneous and non-stable environments, so that there was little chance for steady social analysis and direction of local Catholic life beyond the fundamentals. Thus the problems that the American parishes had to meet almost precluded comprehension on the part of hard-pressed diocesan leaders. A mission Church, facing hostile civic sentiment in a frontier country, was overwhelmed with wave after wave of destitute immigrants whose ignorance and polyglot affiliations daily defied organization. Despite the vast intellectual and administrative resources of Catholicism, the task of rudimentary ecclesiastical development was subject to enormous pressures and interruptions.

These stresses prevented the careful evaluation of the parish in relation to the new urban life. The very size and mobility of the factors involved left many parishes helpless before the onslaught. Yet the conditions of city life must be evaluated by Catholics, and adjustments must be made if the sanctifying functions of the parish are to be carried out.[9]

The Christian community in the cities now contends

not so much with immigrant minority groups as with the new categories of the urban population we have mentioned: the technical and administrative elite which shapes the city by its decisions, the bourgeoisie of wage earners with its materialist ethos and vulnerability to the indoctrination of mass media, and the wretched subproletariat of the slum belts. None of these classes can be neglected in the mission of the parish; each one presents formidable difficulties at every level of religious activity.

The technical and bureaucratic elite is pragmatic in philosophy, generally oblivious of a religious view of society and intent upon the intricacies of scientific practice and "value free" social studies. The position of Catholicism with respect to this elite is at present largely a passive one. The most articulate and talented portions of the Catholic population are not yet influential in these social or professional areas. The time-honored Irish Catholic politician and the other immigrant voting-bloc leaders are usually incompetent either to understand or to deal with the technical elite. More often than not they work to maintain the machine politics of the big cities. Numerous spokesmen have pointed out that the Catholic educational system has not produced its quotas of proficient leaders in various areas of endeavor.[10] Catholic leadership tends to be concentrated in the teaching and legal professions. The clergy, divorced from politics and direct community action in the American Catholic tradition, can play only an indirect role in the formulation of city policy. *Thus Catholic social ideals remain theoretical, and frequently the attitude of the Catholic body social and the formal Catholic institutional network in its relation to city affairs is one of blandly independent self-concern and self-development, with occasional fits of agitated obstructionism.*[11]

The wage-earning bourgeoisie of the city received strong infusions of Catholic population as the immigrant enclaves dissolved under the impact of metropolitan life. In some cities Catholics make up almost two-thirds of the middle-income white-collar and skilled-labor population. This class forms the key personnel of our complex economic system; its skills are the basis of our industrial culture; the technical elite depends upon its support. But the social ideals of this group are still conditioned by a hedonism and a practical secularism which are powerful solvents of religious allegiance. Its behavior patterns are increasingly synthetic—induced by mass communications, fads and demagoguery. Despite the incompatibility between these bourgeois ideals and religious ideals, the influx of large numbers of Catholics has not noticeably affected its mores. *The potential of the Catholic "average American" for joining in a creative reconstruction of our cities has not as yet been manifested in any significant movements at this level.*[12]

In the slums, where social disorder is at its worst, Catholic involvement has declined. The economic improvement of millions of European immigrants through the middle of the 20th century has transferred the infamous distinctions of slum life to populations which are largely Negro and Puerto Rican. Only a small percentage of Negroes are Catholic, and missionary work among the Puerto Rican group is limited. Hence, many Catholic parishes in the older, poorer sections of our cities are maintained by a skeleton crew while the resources of Catholicism shift toward the suburban perimeters of our cities. The plight of the urban subproletariat is disguised by the dimensions of general affluence and the distractions of mechanical life in a mass society. Catholics have fled in growing numbers from the oppressive wastelands of the slums. In doing so, they left hundreds of parishes (which were often just completing the laborious cycle of organization) without communicants—symbols of the dilemma of the modern Christian community, scattering and reforming as the revolutionary city exerts itself.

THE PARISH COMMUNITY

In most urban parishes we are confronted not so much with an emaciated form as with an institution as yet poorly adapted to modern conditions. Catholic analysts have attributed the semi-paralysis of the parochial organization to various causes: lack of reform in the liturgy, which means that for many the message of the Church is not intelligible enough to constitute a spiritual antidote to worldly messages presented more effectively; the expansion and commercialization of the amusement and information media; the sheer size of today's urban parish, which is a formidable barrier to close-knit and stable parochial life. The comment of one experienced priest describes the situation prevalent in big city parishes. In the large urban or suburban parish, "There is a great mass whose only tie is Sunday Mass and the parochial school if they have small children. To the great majority the priest is a whisper behind a blacked-out confessional

screen, a booming voice over a loud speaker, a vague figure at the altar seen from the rear of the church, a func-
tionary when a birth certificate or Mass card is needed
. . . too often he is a stranger—which is strange indeed for
a father."[13] Thus the ideal of a close and paternal relationship of the Christian pastor to his flock is depersonal-
ized in a way which is typical of the relations between the
vast majority of parishioners.

The problems of the densely populated urban parish
are reflected in the defects attending the participation of
Catholics in the central act of worship, the Mass. The individualism of the modern urbanite has shattered the social quality of the participation. The essential nature of
the Holy Sacrifice can never be compromised by the contradictions of human performance, but the mediocrity of
the liturgical execution of this all-important act of prayer
can make a mockery of the *communal* nature of Mass.
The offering of the Mass in many urban parishes is so
rushed, distracted and lacking in dignity that the Mass
can hardly be said to be "celebrated" in any true sense
even on the most joyous Christian feasts. It may be that
an introspective tendency of the urban personality prevents it from unfolding itself in Christian fellowship; the
urbanite, under the impact of constant stimulation, rejects intimacy and deep social participation. Fear of engagement, exposure, involvement is taken into the house
of God where there should be no fear, and where hearts
should be offered readily to effect a unity of love and
simple collaboration in praise of the Lord.

The liturgical problem of the celebration of the Mass in
the urban parish varies, but there are certain constants:

the muteness of the worshippers, their rigid and unthinking observance of set formulas, the conception of the Mass as simply another formal ceremony in a society full of superficial observances. These attitudes prevail even in the urban parishes of smaller size, for pastoral practice tends to follow the norm set by the larger parishes. The larger parishes served by monsignors and bishops have the greatest prestige and influence, and their ministry becomes the model to be imitated. Yet, it is in the larger parishes that the Mass represents the most acute problem.

Lacking a full and satisfying liturgical process, the urban parishes have developed substitutes for participation at Mass. There are novenas, long recitations of trivia about meetings, and ill-prepared sermons that are given by one priest while another priest recites the offertory prayers. These expedients are regarded by the congregation with the same stolid passivity that characterizes the entire Mass attendance. Some lounge and stare; some are intent upon various forms of personal prayer rituals independent of the Mass; some try to follow the rapid Mass with their missals; others, mostly former altar boys, follow at the priest's pace.

Because of the great size of the congregations in many parishes, there is a necessity for discipline in the saying of Masses. But the promptness emphasized to maintain the Mass schedule can be exaggerated. Gospel readings are staccato; sermons are curt. This practice of ministry by timetable and passivity on the part of parishioners becomes routine. Pastors who have the responsibility of serving huge congregations regard the liturgical reform movement with great reserve; the immense problem of educating parishioners to take an adult part in the Mass intimidates them. They have an operating routine, and no desire to change it. As a result, the pronouncements of the Sacred Congregation of Rites in 1958 about the participation of the faithful in the Mass are viewed with a caution which at present prevents reform in many parishes.

What has been said of the Mass applies to other rites, Baptism and Penance for example. Quite commonly, Baptism in the large parish is administered on an assembly-line basis. Infants and godparents are lined up in a row. Perhaps thirty infants are to enter the church that day. The salt is given out to each child in the line; then the blessing with oil; then the affirmation of faith. This is not a coördinated ceremony but a haphazard concession to convenience. The unity of the holy rite is destroyed for those present, and no explanation of the significance of the sacrament is given. The meaningful liturgy of the sacraments is thus transformed into a cold, businesslike and often unintelligible ritual.

The same brusque, routine manner affects the rite of reconciliation, Confession. The sacrament of healing is stereotyped. No counsel is offered; the penance is automatically conferred. That this need not be so can be understood if a penitent goes to one of those large churches where this sacrament is reverently practiced by the members of certain orders. In these churches thousands of confessions are heard daily, yet the disposition of the priests is such that a true sense of healing and assistance is cultivated. In these rites, as in the Mass, the effects of big-city haste, crowding, coldness and lack of gentility

impinge upon the function of the parish. The crudeness
and mechanical method of urbanism have entered the holy
place.

On another level of parish activity the same response
of inertia and ritual observance interferes with the fulfillment of true purpose. Many of the devotional and service
societies persist, not out of their own vitality, but because of official sanction and habit. Often the groups have
no effective program, but simply go through the cus-
tomary activities out of habit. Usually the age level of the
members is high; the groups are sustained by the middle-
aged and elderly. Segregated by sex, they are not con-
genial to the modern American family in which the
husband and wife do things together. Parishes in poor
neighborhoods, with heavy responsibilities of service for
the aged, the ill, the needy, the ignorant, have in so many
cases no adequate corps of workers in the parish societies
to meet these obligations. In the better economic areas
the societies are outpaced by bowling clubs, drive-in
movies, great books discussions, professional societies and
other groups. The Legion of Mary, the Christian Family
Movement, and in some places the St. Vincent de Paul
Society have held their own, but they usually have not
made any decisive change in the spiritual life or the community environment of the parishes.

One of the most awkward features of parish activity is
that of obtaining financial support. On the whole, this
task is accomplished effectively and without any notorious
misfortunes. But in the absence of a fully developed parish life which involves parishioners deeply, fund raising
receives undue notice. Seen, as it often is, out of context,

it becomes too prominent in the minds of the parishioners. The major annual activity of parish societies, perhaps their only intensive one, is likely to be a money-raising party. The parishioner comes to associate the society solely with this function. Raffles, bingo games and drives may be necessary and worthy in themselves, but they often seem to be the only subject of clergy-parishioner communication and sometimes to commercialize the entire life of the parish. Urban emphasis upon pecuniary success has had a strong influence upon parish administration. As one pastor boasted, "Show me a parishioner who is a harder businessman than I am."

If there is one achievement of which the big dioceses of America are proud, it is the parochial school system which instructs hundreds of thousands of Catholic children in the metropolitan areas. This system has been built at an immense cost in money and energy. Today, with the continuing population boom boosting enrollments, the shortage of teachers in religious congregations, rising costs and an increased emphasis on higher education, the Catholic parish schools face another trying time. And just at the time when the parish schools need close attention, there is an equally pressing need for the parish to reshape its adult functions. It has been alleged that the American parish is a child-centered institution which affords no well-planned activities for adults. The schools, which are the largest single undertaking under parish auspices, absorb most of the resources. It seems that in some way the urban and suburban parishes will have to meet the elaborate needs of both children and adults simultaneously or cease to command the traditional support of a

Catholic population which is becoming increasingly middle-class and diversified in its requirements. A careful line must be drawn between social activities and needs and the true spiritual work of the parish. The latter has clear priority, but if it is to be accomplished effectively parallel attention must be paid to meeting social and intellectual needs.

Forced to serve as businessmen, school superintendents, recreation leaders and group organizers, the clergy of the urban parishes have been unable to concentrate on the liturgical, apologetic and counselling functions which should have first call upon their time. Disillusioned with trying to obtain competent lay assistance from among the restricted group of "old faithful" parishioners, most priests have sworn off sharing their parish problems with the laity. Under pressure to get parish work done, they renounce patient collaboration in favor of direct action. In some parishes, the pastor not only never asks advice of parishioners on anything, but makes no financial or debt reports, permits no parent-teacher organization. These pastors maintain a closed operation and rely on their ability to "go it alone," without the interference or committee problems of lay assistance.

The difficulty of simply trying to maintain contact with a parish of eight or ten thousand souls is enormous for the priest. How can he possibly know his flock? As a result of this difficulty he becomes estranged from the families, and the few real contacts, perhaps at a parish party or on the annual visitation of parishioners' homes, are formal and wooden. This distance between the priest and the parishioners is a grave matter. It holds the danger of promoting lay-clergy misunderstanding; for without knowledge of one another, how can the shepherd and his sheep feel the love and affection that bind them together? This problem cannot be solved by cutting back on the responsibilities the parish has assumed. What must be done is to free the priest, the consecrated preacher of the Word and minister of the sacraments, from the lesser tasks of parochial administration. Only in this way can the busy urban parish develop its spiritual life through a deepened application of priestly functions. The laity will somehow have to win enough responsibility through their growth and maturity to look after enough of the burden of administration so that the priest is freed to pursue his higher duties.

The city parish, beset by these various problems, is retarded in its efforts to meet the changes of urbanism or to deal with the more glaring failures of urban community life.

In depressed city areas the difficulty of trying to sustain a Christian community of prayer and fraternity is often overwhelming. In the words of one priest describing his slum parishioners:

They are trapped in social quicksand which drags them down deeper and deeper into the depths of despair. . . . It is this feeling of despair, this sense of frustration, that is too hard to grasp fully . . . the supernatural is built on the natural, yet the intellectual atmosphere breathed in a slum is poisonous to the mind. The inability to grasp the natural virtues makes it difficult to understand the supernatural ones. . . . In the slums as elsewhere the priest is often a lonely figure. He is looked upon as a salesman for a product that people don't want to buy . . .[14]

These conditions are a striking contrast to the theoretical idea of parish life which has been the social ideal of the Catholic Church for two thousand years: "Her doctrine, her liturgy, her prayers, her services are redolent with the spirit of genuine familial union and affection. The primary task of the parish, the molecular unit of ecclesiastical organization, is to evolve the techniques and formulas necessary for the concrete application and demonstration in its group life of this social spirit."[15] It is this familial spirit which is missing amid the individualism and impersonality of the big city.

We would be setting forth a negative and misleading view of parochial life, however, if we did not emphasize the historic achievement that the American parish structure represents. The Church has maintained herself and grown remarkably after starting from a position of weakness. The parishes under her care have nurtured sanctity in high degrees. Utilizing canonical and sacramental means, and building on the conservative peasant traditions of Catholic immigrants, the Church has performed an extraordinary service for American society in her defense of family life. The Catholic school system, unparalleled elsewhere in the world, may be deficient in some ways, but it has added immensely to the civilizing and humanist elements in American life, and its contributions will grow with the passage of time. The charitable works of American Catholicism are impressive and heartening. These attainments have a deep social validity. They are accomplishments in depth, not to be compared with the short-lived "crusades" and "reforms" which have enlivened American social life from time to time. Such social benefits would have been impossible without an active substratum of parochial life. Such conditions as the size of parishes and the mobility and heterogeneity of the life within them must be viewed in relation to these parochial strengths.

Any consideration of the urban parish must also be related to the spheres of Catholic life which have developed outside of parish boundaries as part of the city-wide network of metropolitan life. In most major cities there are dozens of Catholic organizations which have little or no formal connection with parish life. Professional and fraternal groups, missionary associations, lay apostolate groups function without any strict alignment with the parishes. These groups very often represent very perceptive and creative portions of Catholic leadership whose dedication and competence are to be esteemed. The activities and reputation of Catholicism in the general urban community are frequently dependent upon this network of priests and laymen whose careers and interests place them at the center of city life as representatives of the Church. Their achievements or omissions condition the urban milieu in which the parish must function.

We have indicated that Catholic leadership, at least at the level of the dominant technical elite, is deficient in the big cities. We must take note, however, of the accomplishments of Catholic leadership. Although the professional and vocational apostolate is small today, its potential is great. The growing understanding of the liturgical movement within Catholicism is shared by the alert Catholic leaders in the cities. This group is an educational resource and is often in effective contact with the leaders who guide the affairs of the city. The specialized groups of lay apostles in labor, the professions and in key areas of social life are the advance defenses of the parishes against the forces of massive disorganization and secularization.

This network or affiliation of city-wide Catholic leadership is very much a part of the Christian community. It has become detached from the local community and the parish due to urban circumstance, but its involvement with the mainstream of Catholic life is usually intensive. The groups and associations that sustain the leadership network are perhaps too new or too incompletely organized to permit the full elaboration of new Christian community forms and the formation of a strong group tradition. The task of reconciling this indispensable and strategic leadership network with the ancient parochial system or some new mobile form of communal association is one which requires the deepest study.

Because of its numerical and institutional strength, the Catholic population is in a particularly advantageous position to capitalize upon the new currents of reform energy flowing in the urban centers in the mid-twentieth century. The kind of city built under 19th century *laissez faire* capitalism has been repudiated by social leadership. The welfare state has intervened, and the whole concept and technique of "urban renewal" has gained ascendency, with all levels of government experimenting and promoting reconstruction programs.[16] The new professional complex of city planners, architects, urban specialists, administrators and technicians is fast developing.

It is imperative to the mission of the Church in America

that these new currents of energy be guided by a sound social philosophy. The new profession of urban rebuilder must be penetrated by many competent and apostolically-minded Catholics. It is evident that this whole movement is weakest in the area of social policy and basic goals. This may be a vacuum which Catholic social thought could help to fill. In any event we simply cannot ignore a movement which presents an opportunity of such great portent.

The correction and restoration of urban life in America has world-wide implications. Barbara Ward has noted of the tendency toward mass life:

> If you go and see a new workers' suburb, whether it is in Cairo, or on the outskirts of Bombay, or out in Australia, or again in America, the type of architecture, the type of housing, the big blocks of flats all tend to be the same; and in whichever country you are there is a remarkable resemblance between steel plants. And again and again one has the sense that the twentieth century contribution to this world is constantly the same, is constantly reinforcing a kind of mass background, a mass environment, and that if you want variety you must look back to the things that have been created in the past.[17]

American social leadership must be made manifest to a world that is fast urbanizing. If the Christian and democratic nations like the United States cannot control and make socially wholesome the immense energies of industrial urbanism, then their way of life will hardly gain the allegiance of those who are skeptical of or opposed to both Christianity and democracy.

There is evidence that Catholic leaders are beginning

to perceive the relationship between the Christian parish community and these movements. Pioneers in Catholic social action were certainly conscious of the great social changes which their work implied if the new industrial culture was to be penetrated. The analyses of such men as Reverend Joseph Fichter, S.J., Reverend Joseph Fitzpatrick, S.J., of Fordham University, and Reverend François Houtart of Louvain University, who studied Chicago parishes, have initiated a discussion which will inevitably grow to be one of the major concerns of the Church in America in future decades. Father Fichter has asserted that "the urban parish, in most instances, has long ago ceased to be a group, in the technical meaning of a group. It's becoming something of an enterprise in which most lay people do not have any close relations, and do not perform essential functions. . . . The urban parish is breaking up."[18]

Judgments such as this must be contrasted with the continuing conviction that the geographical parish is essential to the religious life of the Church. The solution to the question of the relative efficiency of the territorial parish versus some new form of pastoral care will probably be a mixed one, and it will not be easily attained.[19] There are parochial administrative changes already well underway which have critically altered the structure of the parish. Most of these changes involve the participation of the laity.[20]

The parish of the future will also be affected by the growth of social science and its employment by Catholics. The study of the sociology of religion has become an accepted part of diocesan administration in some countries such as Belgium, Holland and France. The relationships between social studies, town and city planning and administration are growing, and Catholics will profit by utilizing the techniques and findings of the social sciences. In the United States this development is not widely felt, but it has great significance for the future.

THE RESPONSIBILITY OF THE LAITY

The active participation of the laity in reform of the parish is an outgrowth of the Catholic Action movement launched by Pope Pius XI. Admittedly, strong lay support and collaboration are a prerequisite of Catholic social stability in urban society, but there are grave problems involved. As Father Fichter says: ". . . one of the greatest obstacles to restructuring of lay organizations in urban parishes seem to lie in the traditional relationship between priest and people. In most instances, initiative and authority lie firmly in the hands of the priests, and this is probably because ultimate responsibility is also the priest's. The principle of self-direction and of lay responsibility basic to the modern concept of the organized lay apostolate, runs contrary to this tradition."[21] The future of the lay apostolate, however, seems assured. The Papacy, the majority of the Church's intellectual leaders, and the most creative groups working for social justice form a heartening phalanx committed to the movement and intent upon its extension and success.

It would not be fanciful to say that the entire problem of the Church in the modern world is reflected in the struggle for social integrity in the urban parish. It is as if the allegory of the "City of God" and the "City of Man" of St. Augustine had been revived in very concrete terms. Churchmen such as Cardinal Suhard and Cardinal Saliège have analyzed the historical issues; others, such as Abbé Michonneau in his book *Revolution in a City Parish,* have made specific the tasks which must be performed at the parochial level. As Cardinal Suhard wrote: "It is a question of building the new world, of specifying and preparing the structures which will enable man to be fully man, in a city worthy of him, of transforming all things to make of them a Christian world."[22]

For American Catholics this transformation necessarily involves the urban milieu with its technical complexity. "The chief contribution of Catholicism to intellectual life in North America," says psychiatrist Karl Stern, "will in the time to come center around the conflict of humanism versus technocracy."[23] It is in the modern city that this conflict between human and divine values and the dehumanizing aspects of technology is most urgent.

As the Church defended freedom against Roman tyrants, medieval kings and liberal autocrats, she must contend for the moral and psychological liberty of men against the uncontrolled influences of the technical city. This means that her communities must avoid the anarchy of individualism as well as the degradation of crude collectivism in developing Christian social life.

Within an urban social order partially sustained by Christian community life, at least some of the citizens can find liberty in their surrender to God. At the same time such citizens can give their lives to the community unreservedly, for they will see that the community offers the opportunity of a daily spiritual dialogue with Christ. If there are enough citizens inspired by this ideal, our urban society may have the necessary quota of "just" men to restore it. Father John Courtney Murray, S.J. has aptly expressed the goal of the Christian community in city life: "Love of the city's common good, with the faith in goodness that it implies, is itself a form of the love of the true God who is Goodness itself; this is so, whatever the strenuously agnostic secularist may say. And if this be so, how shall Christian faith in Christ, the Son of God and one-time citizen of earth, not be the dynamic principle of a great love of the city's common good."[24]

There is a penalty to be paid for failure to defend the freedom of men in the Christian parish and in other groups in our society. "To destroy or diminish the reality of the smaller areas of society, to abolish or restrict the range of cultural alternatives offered individuals in economic endeavor, religion and kinship, is to destroy in time the roots of the will to resist despotism in its larger forms."[25]

THE MYSTICAL BODY

This temporal penalty, however, is dwarfed by the awful tragedy of the moral and religious losses incurred by masses of men in the modern world. The souls of men are the prizes sought in the social struggles of our era. It was for this reason that what is perhaps the most profound, fundamental and socially significant of the modern Papal encyclicals was written. The encyclical *Mystici Corporis* summarizes the religious meaning that suffuses all of society. It is this meaning and intelligibility, one might even say it is the Word, that is at stake in a crucial way in the revolutionary city. The worship of the Word, and all the conditions—political, economic, social, psychological and moral—which make that worship possible, must be defended. To take away the social expression of worship or liturgy "is a public misfortune and its suppression is the extreme punishment with which God threatens cities, 'I will cause to cease in this place the voice of the bridegroom and the voice of the bride.' " (Jerem. vii, 34).

The encyclical summary of Catholic teaching about the inhabitation of the world by Christ is deceptive in its brevity and simplicity. The *Encyclical on the Mystical Body* is more than a theological treatise. Part of the body of Papal literature drawn up as the first full-scale response of Catholicism to the problems of the modern era, it is a statement of a most compelling set of social premises. And yet its teaching has not yet been emphatically displayed in the mores and practices of modern Christians; the formal agencies of doctrinal exposition seem to be at a loss to transmit its profound significance.

The doctrine that Christ lives on in the lives of His faithful upon earth is an ancient Christian belief rooted in the New Testament, particularly in Pauline teaching. The doctrine has been retaught by one Church Father after another. Successive generations are preoccupied with different dogmas. At one time in the West, the Nativity was such a preoccupation, and the Franciscans brought new perspective into Christian understanding of the teaching. In the East the Resurrection was the occasion of a similar devotion and distinction. But the social elaboration of the teaching of the Mystical Body has not been achieved in the same way. Whatever the promptings of the Holy Spirit with respect to such a process, it does seem that rationally no more fruitful development could be desired.

The doctrine of the indwelling presence of Christ in His members has a special relevance to the mass society and accelerating population of our century. We are living in the day of the physical unification of mankind through technology and rapid communications. This unification cannot be a mechanical thing; it must be carried out in spiritual as well as physical terms. Only an Infinite God, present to all the millions in an intimate way, can bind them together.

In the mass cities there must be some ideal that gives significance to the rushing crowds, the feverish collaboration and the tension. What is more meaningful than the presence of Christ in man? Through the presence of Christ that man is made unique; his life is defended from the anonymity of the neuter welter of technically driven trivia and is bound to the lives of others by a sympathy and an understanding which only an omniscient Creator can confer upon a beloved creature.

The reality of the Mystical Body of Christ thus has significance for the particular social milieu in which the city man finds himself, but it has even more pertinence to the spiritual attitudes of the modern world. It is with respect to the ultimate spiritual dispositions of the urban elite that the doctrine is most clearly efficacious. Consider first the import of this doctrine for the naturalism which is a cardinal theme of urban psychology. The excessive pride of human nature which tempts it to do without the supernatural is, like all great errors, a perversion of a fundamental truth. The deification of man cannot be countered by debasing man and demeaning his role in creation. Rather, the antidote for the naturalism which accords man a false autonomy by placing him at the pinnacle of a half-world of "purely natural" phenomena is to stress the true dignity of man, the heir of heaven, seen in the light of Christ's redemption. By affirming the dignity of eternal life, the beginning of which is the spiritual experience of man on earth, the position and work of modern man can be placed in perspective. The inflated eminence of modern man shrinks and he is seen to be dependent on grace. The vain portrait of man as the omnipotent master of the natural realm is seen as a fraud upon man's true dignity and mission.

The projection of the fullness of the Mystical Body into modern history would also refute the liberal individualism which has atomized social relations in the urban centers. Individualist egotism in response to the pressures of mass life is an anarchic influence in the life of cities. Constructing a unity of social life on the premises of Christ incarnate in His people would overcome this alienation. If the brittle egotism of the besieged modern personality could be modified, there would be less pathology vented in the destructive politics and nationalism which periodically sweep urban society. The human person would not be so prone to rely upon itself for fulfillment, but would find itself enriched and amplified in unity with the "becoming" of God's living Will.

Finally, this glorious doctrine provides a remedy for the false conceptions of society which seek to strengthen some social groups by sacrificing the rights of others. The principle of respecting the integrity of smaller social groups is strongly stated in the Papal teachings on the reconstruction of the social order. The teaching about the Mystical Body provides the sanction for this principle and complements it with a theological justification.

Although the Encyclical on the Mystical Body is related most especially to the visible structure of the Church, the effects of the doctrine cannot be so circumscribed. All mankind is affected; all history embraced. It is with assurance, then, that we can relate the specific problems of urban life and spirituality to this teaching.

NOTES

1. "The Rock," from *The Complete Poems and Plays of T. S. Eliot* (New York: Harcourt Brace & Co., 1952), p. 101.
2. E. A. Gutkind, *op. cit.*, p. 32.
3. H. P. Douglass, *The City's Church* (New York: Friendship Press, 1929). See also E. R. Hooker, *Hinterlands of the Church* (New York: Institute of Social and Religious Research, 1931) and F. S. Chapin "The Protestant Church in an Urban Environment" in *Contemporary American Institutions* (New York: Harper and Brothers, 1935).
4. K. D. Miller, *Man and God in the City* (New York: Friendship Press, 1955).
5. Gilbert Beaver, *Christ and Community* (New York: Association Press, 1950).
6. Reinhold Niebuhr, "Piety and Secularism in America," *The Atlantic Monthly* (Anniversary Issue, 1957).

7. Bernard I. Bell, *Crowd Culture* (Chicago: Henry Regnery Co., 1952), p. 22.

8. C. J. Nuesse and T. J. Harte, *The Sociology of the Parish* (Milwaukee: Bruce Publishing Co., 1951), p. 43.

9. H. A. Reinhold, *The American Parish and the Roman Liturgy* (New York: Macmillan Co., 1958), p. 128.

10. See for example John Tracy Ellis, "American Catholics and the Intellectual Life," in *Thought* (Autumn, 1955).

11. In a study of the "Moral Integration of American Cities" in *Cities and Society*, ed. by Paul Hatt and Albert Reiss (Glencoe, Illinois: The Free Press, 1957), Robert C. Angell indicated that church membership has less influence on the social life of cities than such factors as mobility, occupational patterns and property tenure.

12. Christopher Dawson, "Catholicism and the Bourgeois Mind," in *Dynamics of World History* (New York: Sheed and Ward, 1957), p. 200.

13. Rev. Dennis J. Geaney, in *Worship* (December, 1956).

14. "Priest of the Slums" (Anonymous) in *The Commonweal* (August 24, 1956).

15. C. J. Nuesse and T. J. Harte, *The Sociology of the Parish, loc. cit.*, p. 152.

16. The stirrings of city renewal, largely confined to center city redevelopment of commercial areas, are described by Hal Burton in *The Cities Fight Back* (New York: Citadel Press, 1954).

17. Barbara Ward in *The Commonweal* (November 28, 1952).

18. Quoted in *Ave Maria* (June 15, 1957).

19. Rev. H. A. Reinhold states this necessity for a "mixed solution" in *The American Parish and the Roman Liturgy, loc. cit.* There are various examples of changing parochial structure. A British researcher, Mr. Anthony Spencer, head of the Newman Demographic Survey, has suggested a flexible pastoral form to cope with city-wide needs. See *The London Tablet*, "Planning Parishes" (June 7, 1958). St. Richard's parish in Minneapolis has tried to organize geographic sub-groups. See *Jubilee* (August 1958). A Parish in Himeji, Japan, has also tried geographical subdivision as a solution to problems grow-

ing out of size and density of population. See "Neighborhood Associations" in *Worship* (December 1956).

20. Peter Drucker, "The Management Audit of the Catholic Church" in *America* (February 26, 1956). "The modern big city diocese and big city parish are outgrowing a traditional managerial pattern and organizational structure."

21. Joseph Fichter, S.J., *Social Relations in the Urban Parish* (Chicago: University of Chicago Press, 1954), p. 163.

22. Emmanuel Cardinal Suhard, *Growth or Decline* (Chicago: Fides Publishers, 1948), pp. 82-83.

23. Karl Stern, Address at Rosary College, River Forest, Illinois, 1958. NCCM news release.

24. John Courtney Murray, S.J., in *The Annals of the American Academy of Political and Social Science* (March 1948), p. 41.

25. Robert Nisbet, *The Quest for Community, loc. cit.*, p. 202.

5. The Christian Response

The Essentials of Urban Renewal
A Christian Program
The Role of the Lay Apostolate
Human Conditions of Life

The Christian Response

THE ESSENTIALS OF URBAN RENEWAL

"The city," says St. Thomas, "is in fact the most important thing instituted by human reason. For it is the object of all lesser communities."[1] The *civitas* which St. Thomas had in mind was, of course, the *polis* of Aristotle, a small, intimate society rather than an urban conglomeration. The ancient thinkers were aware of the importance of that level of social affairs where life was still organically interrelated and continuous, and not so heavily dependent upon juridical fiat, abstractions and bureaucracy. The real form of a city is much more an equilibrium of naturally related groups than it is a system of technical powers and legalities, however important these latter features may be. In an age of nationalism we have tended in most of our social judgments to overvalue the state and to neglect the significance of those social forms such as the city which are anterior to it. Thus, the city has lost its form and the nation state hovers over a society composed of bewildered individuals and inharmonious groups caught in the throes of social revolution.

Yet, if men are to lead wholesome lives, the integrity

of such social forms as the city must be restored. The accidental congregation of divers elements, unplanned technical extension, greed and needless complexity must be overcome in the interests not only of order but of true freedom. In modern society the city must serve two portentous purposes. It must be the organ of a great society and it must be democratic. Our urban life must sustain the mass population, industrial processes and vitality of a society with constantly expanding horizons; it must also provide the orderly civic experience of democratic responsibility, for the only alternatives to self-rule in a mass society are chaos or despotism.

The role of Christians in reforming urban life in a pluralistic society must be a partial one. Nevertheless, the role of Christians in reshaping city life is critical. The Christian understanding of social life provides the only resource adequate to the Promethean task of imprinting spiritual meaning upon the world of urban technology. No humanist formula will suffice in itself; the problem is too great. Failure will lead to a sanitary serfdom such as George Orwell imagined for "1984." We already have examples of the tyranny of urban bureaucratic systems. The Soviets have built new cities beyond the Urals and rebuilt Stalingrad after World War II at a revolting price of forced labor and coercion; South Africa is rebuilding Johannesburg according to plans based upon racist megalomania; Latin American dictators build splendid office skyscrapers and hotels while hundreds of thousands of people live wretchedly in tin-roofed hovels. Careful planning and technology alone will not master the whirlwind of urban social change. Only leadership which transcends the immediate time will have sufficient perspective; only leadership bent upon sacrifices and seeing the image of God in man will be able to refine a good city out of the machine world of our century.

Because of the minority position of Christians and of Catholics, their leadership in urban restoration must be collaborative and of the highest competence. This point cannot be affirmed too strongly. Civic organization and reform require common effort. Christians must earn the confidence and assistance of their colleagues in a pluralist society not only by their undeniable and selfless devotion to the common good, but by their insistence upon excellence in every phase of urban professional life and civic renovation. Only by providing openly coöperative leadership can Christians avoid stultifying separatism or ineffectual piecemeal efforts. This task of obtaining broad support for Christian plans is the first great problem to be faced by Catholics intent upon reconstructing urban life.

In order to obtain a favorable climate of opinion for social policies in our society the Christian minority must be prepared to have every proposal it makes questioned and proven on the basis of its merit. This places an immense demand upon the initiative and persuasiveness of Christian leaders. Consent cannot be coerced. Only the most purely motivated social leadership will communicate the enthusiasm necessary to obtain public support.

Second to the problem of obtaining support for Christian ideals in a pluralist society, the problem of circumscribing urbanism with some rational social limits is most critical. No civic order can be organized unless the present reckless fluidity of city development is curbed. In many major cities it is almost impossible to tabulate the expansion. In such cases, what can be said of the ability of those in responsible positions to evaluate the radiating social effects of physical changes? In order to control urban and suburban development, there must be a public commitment to order. Without this commitment the whims of individualism and the propulsion of unregulated technology will thrust the city into courses of development that are entirely accidental and frequently detrimental.

In the interests of the Christian concepts of the dignity of man and the primacy of rational social direction, Catholics should insist that limits be devised for urban growth. This position has been made quite clear in Catholic comment on industrial problems. Pius XII in 1947 made this view explicit: "The Church wants some limits set to the dwarfing of man himself in these days through the emergence and dominance of the machine and the continued expansion of large scale industry."[2]

The Bishops of Australia have made a clear application of this point of view to the difficult problems posed by the concentration of the Australian population in large cities.[3] These Church leaders firmly endorsed decentralization and the principle of the limitation of the size of any one city. Supporting the judgment of men relying on philosophical reasons is the opinion of a growing number of technicians that a limit must be placed on the size and population of the city.[4]

Fortunately, statistics on growth ratios to be expected in different kinds of urban areas are increasingly available and reliable and will help to make this kind of planning possible. This will be the first step toward control of size. It has been argued that all of the modern services which make urbanism so attractive can be provided in technical-industrial cities of between 100,000 and 200,000 persons.[5] We may, indeed, hope and work for a day when the oppression of the congested monster cities of the early industrial age will be as much a thing of the past as the oppression which nature once exercised over man.

If the problems of an enlightened urban opinion and the designation of rational limits for the metropolis can be resolved, Christians will be free to pursue the restoration of urbanism according to their ideals. In doing so they will profit from the plans of urban renewal advanced by so many brilliant contemporary architects. The works of the critics and utopians who fought to redirect industrial urban life are instructive both in their positive vision of new city forms and in their failure to achieve urban reforms. Beginning in the last century with the work of William Morris and John Ruskin and continuing with the original ideas of Patrick Geddes, Sir Raymond Unwin, Ebenezer Howard and Le Corbusier, the movement for the renewal of cities has fought against the excesses of technology and the dead weight of civic apathy.[6]

In the United States the "City Beautiful" movement in the first decades of this century strove for a limited urban rebuilding, relying largely upon aesthetics or inspiration. Imposing public buildings and formal gardens were erected as part of monumental plans which hardly touched the residential or industrial portions of the cities. Later plans for "greenbelt communities," "satellite towns" and other proposals for the construction of completely new urban areas emphasized decentralization and the concept of the residential neighborhood as a traffic-free, self-contained entity. With the extension of the activities of the welfare state, many of these new urban forms were experimentally built under government auspices and helped to bring about improvements in physical planning which curbed the worst profiteering in urban land and construction. They have paved the way for revision of the construction industry and the techniques of community building. The movement for city planning and renewal reached something of a high point when one city after another appointed planning bodies with professional staffs.

The pressure of population and the dynamic quality of American economic life, however, have outstripped the infant operations of public planning bodies. In particular, static legal boundaries which the cities inherited from the last century have blocked public control of the expanding metropolitan developments. Many planners have abdicated, outraged at public indifference, the meager powers granted to planning bodies, and the suspicion that this type of control is one more form of creeping socialism.[7]

Thus hopes for renewal of our urban areas are still little more than abstract schemes and architects' sketches, and city planners have become preoccupied with the bread-and-butter projects involving slum clearance and highways while the broader features of city reconstruction are deferred and eventually abandoned.

Among the chief handicaps which have retarded the promotion of a true city order has been the lack of widely accepted community standards and goals of civic consensus in another connection. In the field of city planning, this deficiency in social thinking is symbolized by the long-standing alienation between professional planners and social scientists. The city-planning fraternity pretends to be even more "value free" than the social scientist, and is so fearful of the onus of being "authoritarian" in a democratic society that it has divorced itself as far as possible from social judgment. On the other hand, rather than begin the tedious process of consultation with the public in order to stimulate conscious social guidance, the planners have affected a "value free" aloofness while making decisions with profound social implications in one program after another.

A mildly interested public is regularly shown attractive models and Sunday supplement descriptions, but it has not up till now been very thoughtful about programs of city renewal. The major reason for the failure of urban reconstruction programs has been this want of public support.[9] The lack of popular support of renewal plans and the wholly mechanical and superficial character of many of the plans themselves are twin reflections of the social weakness which afflicts the life of the revolutionary city. The energy of this city is so much more mechanistic than human that human guidance has become a rarity. Those responsible for the task of rebuilding have been unable, because of their own confusion and the apathy of the public, to summon a mandate for civic reorganization from a disorganized society.

While the solution to the problems of urbanism depends upon a philosophical inquiry into the ultimate ends of new social processes, any new philosophy of urbanism must be implemented in the practical order. Answering

questions about the fulfillment of man's nature in the
metropolis, the nature of technical achievement and the
role of social change in human life will not effect the reform of civic institutions. What are needed are operative
principles for social action derived from sound philosophy.
Then the norms and principles of social reconstruction
must be related to the changing forces shaping urban
life; there should be no fear of charges of utopianism.

All that I have written indicates that American Catholics cannot remain passive while the new world-shaping
force of technical urbanism expands and deepens its
power over modern social life. It must be re-emphasized
that the United States is the foremost exponent of this
type of urban development, and American Catholics are
a predominantly urban people. This combination of circumstances places an extraordinary responsibility and opportunity before the American Catholic population. The
tempest of technical urbanism must be controlled in ac-
cordance with Christian principle. Already whole sections
of the non-Western world are poised to imitate the models
of urban life which are offered to them by the Western
industrial countries. It is, therefore, appropriate for us to
consider at this point some of the actions to be taken to
provide a program of Christian social leadership under
Catholic auspices which will assume the initiative in
urban affairs.

A CHRISTIAN PROGRAM

Any program of Christian social leadership in city life
will have to determine what standards, methods and

forms are desirable for the urban society in which we live, and it will have to secure their endorsement and development through education. Experiments will be necessary to make new plans for urban life concrete and widely applied. The aim of all these efforts will be to build an urban society which will afford the ordinary citizen the chance to pursue his salvation in conditions that are not debasing and exploitive, but humane and encouraging.

1. *The first need is for a Christian social policy relating to modern urbanism.* In order to arrive at this policy, Christian social principles concerning such issues as the extent of government authority, social opportunity, cultural pluralism, and the subsidiarity of social groups and functions will have to be re-appraised in the light of their application to urban conditions. The impressive technical and social studies of urban life, which have been compiled largely by non-Catholics, will require analysis and interpretation so that any Christian policies or programs will be based upon as broad a knowledge of social fact as possible. Although urban social study is only one phase of all social study, and academicians would decry special emphasis upon it, in the practical order urbanism respects no textbook limitations in its scope and must be given priority for analysis. A concerted program of research into urban conditions, particularly in the field of the sociology of religion, is greatly needed. The labor of obtaining an undistorted social picture of modern city life would be a service of inestimable value not only to the Church in her mission but to American society as a whole.

For this purpose, Christian orientated study centers devoted to analyzing city affairs should be established.

Support for such centers could come from Catholic universities, the hierarchy and branches of the lay apostolate. These centers could coördinate study projects, maintain libraries and publish findings which would be the basis for public discussion and governmental action. Staffed by expert and dedicated men, such Christian study centers on urban affairs could lay the intellectual groundwork for the social apostolate directed at the revolutionary city.

In the design of a social policy for urbanism Catholics have the advantages of a long tradition of social experience, a body of social teaching adapted to modern conditions by a succession of brilliant Papal leaders, and a universal institutional life which has made an amazing recovery from the secular restrictions placed upon it in the 19th century.

Modern Christian social teaching has been forthright and clear about the problems of industrialism which are central to the revolutionary city. In their defense of the human person and the family, the modern Popes have been unrelenting, and often virtually alone amid bitter critics of the Christian ethic. In fields connected with residential and community life, however, the implications of the social encylicals and other teaching are not clear. It must be the aim of Christians involved in city life to evolve an exposition of the social teachings of the Church with respect to our novel urban situation. This kind of application has been tried, with real achievement, in villages of the Dutch Coöperative Movement, the projects of Léon Harmel in France and the factories of Alan Turner's Spa Lane Mills.

2. *The second phase of a Christian program for restora-*

tion of city life would consist of a broad educational effort utilizing all of the institutions and media available to the Church. At the college and university level, courses must be organized to include a presentation of the Christian position in a contemporary context and in relation to modern city life. This is particularly pertinent to social studies and the humanities, but the issue must be posed also in the technical fields and in the study of religion and ethics. The direction of students into such fields as architecture, city planning, public administration and social work is extremely important.[10]

There are two levels on which an educational program about Christian responsibilities in the modern city is most gravely needed. One is in the area of guidance of the professional and civic personnel who are Christians, but who are unclear about the course to pursue in the world of community problems. A rigorous and expert system of guidance for such elements must be organized either through vocational groupings or through a sustained series of seminars, study weeks or professional inquiries. Centers of influence similar in orientation to Father Ricardo Lombardi's training institute of his Movement for a Better World in Italy are needed to focus interest upon urbanism. The International Movement of Catholic Intellectuals and such groups as the Young Christian Workers provide excellent networks for exchange and the vocational formation of Christians for the urban apostolate.

The other area where counselling and an intensive evaluation of urban prospects are needed is in the sphere of the parish and local Catholic institutions. Diocesan administrators, pastors and intelligent laymen must be brought to see the parish as part of a fabric of social life which has been torn by the disruptive force of city changes. Special lectures in seminaries and the use of such organized groups as the Cardinal's Committee on Neighborhood Conservation in Chicago will help to inform the clergy of municipal projects and urban trends.

The encouragement of lay participation and leadership in community organization, urban renewal activities and community service will not be easy. Special adult education media would undoubtedly be the central feature of the promotion of Christian lay knowledge of city life. The experiments of Father Joseph Gremillion and Father Marvin Bordelon in their informal and timely "Collegium" in a suburban Shreveport, Louisiana, parish show what can be done along these lines.[11] The lethargy of decades must be overcome. Not only must a new vision of community life be held out to Catholic citizens to inspire them to civic reconstruction, but this vision must lead to a distinctive Christian contribution to city life. Such a contribution would mean revival of the concept and practice of civic virtue in a Christian sense. The educational task of fostering such a revival is an enormous and obviously a long-range one, but the established Catholic educational system can be invaluable.

3. *The fruit of a renewed spirit of Christian civic enlightenment will be harvested in a program of urban social action aimed at creating a new society in a new kind of city.* The achievements of reform and social invention in this field are dependent not so much upon obtaining more schools or housing or open space as upon an exertion of talent, character, and leadership on the part of

individuals. This fact does not diminish the magnitude of the purely technical activity which must be undertaken; population studies, economic planning, land-use plans and housing-and-neighborhood-renewal efforts must be studied because of the social import of decisions in these areas.

THE ROLE OF THE LAY APOSTOLATE

In order to be sure that Christains assume their share of responsibility for decisions in the areas just noted, it will be necessary for the urban *layman* to exercise his apostolate with astuteness. The past record of failure to organize vocational groups for laymen in the new administrative and technical professions will have to be overcome.[12] Unless a sense of Christian mission can be infused into the white-collar and executive vocations related to the control of urban affairs, there will be no reconstitution of city life. The same old impersonality, individualism, exploitation and indifference will prevail. The vocational areas which are particularly important for Christian orientation and Catholic action techniques are those embracing local government, city planning and architecture, community organization and welfare and those positions in private industry dealing with such works as housing and transportation. The influence of Christian guilds of technicians and executives in these areas is indispensable to the reconstitution of urban society. Only men fully aware of Christian social values and in positions of influence will be able to counteract the impetus toward giantism in the revolutionary city.

The experience of American Catholics in organizing their huge educational system and in working in the labor movement will provide a background for the organization of social action in urban affairs. Indeed, what the struggle to obtain decent working conditions was to Catholics in the first several decades of this century, the struggle to regenerate urban society may be in the second half of the century. In the beginning, the targets of Catholic social action will probably be determined rather accidentally; eventually, however, the apostolate must be purposefully oriented toward the tasks which confront it with some logical social priority.

In the United States, it seems, the lay apostolate has achieved its most effective status outside the more formal lines of Church authority. In the last fifty years two influences have strongly conditioned the lay apostolate in this country and left their mark upon a perceptive portion of the laity in terms of experience and outlook.

First is the influence which may be called "the rural life tendency." Practically all attempts at building Christian forms of community life in the United States have been wedded to a preference for rural life. Many apostolic Catholic families, in rebellion against oppressive urban forces, have turned toward rural life as conscious pioneers hoping to provide a witness to the coöperative, integrated, holy life possible on the land. The experiments and activities of the rural life apostles were some of the very first testimonials to the boldness of the Catholic laity in a largely heedless 20th century America. In many ways they prepared the ground for current developments of the lay apostolate.

A second influence has been the proximate needs of social action which have confronted the laity, quite often taking it unaware. Emergencies have created Catholic groups to deal with them. The National Catholic Welfare Conference, for example, was a response to problems which were an outgrowth of World War I. The Catholic Worker Movement, the Association of Catholic Trade Unionists, the Catholic Interracial Councils and many other groups grew up almost spontaneously to meet pressing problems which long cried out for attention.

Much of the lay apostolate, therefore, is not grounded on any planned deployment of resources, but rather upon needs which have accidentally arisen in the historical course of events. Whatever may be said of this development in its aspects of democracy and enthusiasm, the question of what problems have precedence for Catholicism in the urban social order have not been clearly defined.

With respect to the problems that face the urban Christian Father François Houtart has written:

Religious life, like human behavior in general, is influenced by the functional sphere in which man works and spends a great part of his life. It is, therefore, important, even essential, for the religious life of the masses, that the whole environment of their lives should be oriented in a Christian direction. If not, it will be an active element in their de-Christianizaton. . . . Obviously the parochial organization as such does not provide the answer. The only solution would be to train the laity, enabling them to assume the charge and control of their institutions and environment. . . . However, it must be acknowledged that a response suited to the transformation which modern society has undergone and which the fact of urbanization, in particular, illustrates is lacking. Actually this demands a veritable revolution in the concept of the apostolate.[13]

Father Houtart designates four areas which he feels have a special claim upon Christian attention in social affairs: the urban parish, the residential or "living" environment, race relations and the rural parish.[14]

The urban Catholic is faced in most major cities with a vast non-white population, largely depressed and chiefly non-Catholic. This may well be the first practical task facing the Church in the work of urban reconciliation. There is hardly a chancery office in the great industrial centers today which is not surrounded in the older core of its city by the persistent "American dilemma" of race relations. For the first time in North America the Church faces the race question on a huge numerical scale in the very strongest centers of Catholic development. The work of the Catholic Interracial Councils in such cities as Chicago, New York and St. Louis has made a beginning in meeting this problem, but their work has been extremely circumscribed and very slow in relation to the great numbers of racial changes which have taken place.

HUMAN CONDITIONS OF LIFE

The social action phase of the Christian apostolate of city life must be thoroughly interwoven with the apostolates of family life and the parish community. The residential community, where personal and family life is enacted in all its intimacy, has a certain priority. At the local community level, it is housing which is the key factor in the matrix of neighborhood life. Unless the residential and domestic character of the local community can be established through the liberation of housing accommodations from detrimental influences, family life and community vitality are bound to suffer. Housing gravely affects family life. As Pope Pius XII has said: "Only that stability that is rooted in one's own holding makes of the family the most vital and most perfect and fruitful cell of society. . . . If today the concept of the creation of vital spaces is at the center of social and political aims, should not one, before all else, think of the vital space of the family and free it from the fetters of conditions which do not permit even the formulation of the idea of a homestead of one's own. . . . These requirements (of social justice) include provision for the people of the necessary houses. . . . Can there be conceived a social need of greater urgency?"[15] If housing is important to family life, it is also usually the greatest single physical factor affecting the social composition and temporal situation of the urban parish. This fact is little understood by many otherwise well-informed Christian leaders. It is essential that the revival of urban life grow out of a renewal of residential life, but in this area of activity the social scene is strewn with the wreckage of dozens of well-intentioned programs.

Despite the headlines and conferences which have kept housing matters before the public, the relationship of this extremely important area of social decisions to the social teaching of the Catholic Church has been only vaguely realized and only weakly publicized. During the 1930's

there were various Catholic commentators like Msgr.
John A. Ryan, who publicly scored poor housing conditions and advocated reforms, but the glow of middle-
class prosperity seems to have taken the edge off Catholic
social action in this matter.

Today, it seems, we are too contented with planning
parking lots and gymnasiums to attend to the vital housing problems which can so easily and drastically affect
the size, morale, health and opportunities of thousands
of families. Occasionally we will read a news story carrying the remarks on housing of such remarkable men as
Archbishop Robert E. Lucey of San Antonio or Msgr.
John O'Grady of the National Conference of Catholic
Charities, but there is practically no comment on national
housing issues by Catholic laymen. Considering that housing is a hotly controversial subject with great social significance, and that there are probably hundreds of
thousands of Catholics directly involved in the housing
industry in one way or another, the lack of expression is
incredible.

There is no sustained apostolate of study and activity
devoted to this field. The American Church does not have
such vivid examples of Christian concern in this area as
the two movements that have captured so much attention
in Europe: the provision of homes for displaced persons
through Father Dominic Pire's Europe of the Heart
(which won the Nobel Peace Prize for 1958) and the
Building Brothers group which has put up hundreds of
structures in recent years under the auspices of the Nober-
tine fathers.

Some few efforts to make new departures toward solv-

ing housing needs have stood out because of their boldness and their isolation in a sea of indifference. The
families at Marycrest near Nyack, New York, who stub-
bornly built their own homes; St. Louis builder Charles
Vatterott, who built homes for Negroes in defiance of
prevailing practices; the protests of a few New York City
pastors against slum conditions in West Manhattan—
these are rare examples. But the pronouncements of a
few resolute priests and bishops are no substitute for
genuine widespread concern among Catholics.

The lack of a planned apostolate in housing at the national level has meant that there has been little Catholic
opinion represented in the shaping of legislation and
housing programs since the adoption of the Wagner Housing Act of the 1930's. Housing is a technical field. To be
meaningful, influence must be based upon competence
and an understanding of the immensely complex forces
of the market, the construction industry and population
trends. Catholic social action leaders, whose ranks are
very thin today, seldom have a good knowledge of these
complexities.

Whole new concepts are under consideration and actual
nation-wide programs such as urban renewal and industrial decentralization are in progress. Catholic social
teaching remains isolated from these dynamic areas of
social change, and will continue to have little influence
until some vehicles are built to develop Chrsitian interest
in housing and related matters both on the local and
national levels.

The outline for improvement of housing conditions
should be familiar to most intelligent citizens. There has

been long, and often heated, discussion of the issue. New housing and zoning regulations for municipalities, wise use of government subsidies and insurance of mortgages, the adoption of new technology and building techniques by the housing industry, and many other important steps have been recommended time and again. Controversy has raged about public housing, equal opportunity in the housing market for minority groups, and a great variety of proposals for bringing about better housing for various segments of the population. Most experts agree that there are several general reforms that must accompany any national program for rebuilding of the country's housing and the provision of "a decent home in a good environment for every American family." These are:

1. *The reorganization of the housing industry into a more coherent and economically stable production system.* Heretofore, the construction industry has been characterized by cyclical fluctuations, technological lag and an inability to meet the needs of low-income families, large families and minority families. The industry is split into warring tribes of mortgage lenders, material suppliers, builders, trade unions and real estate brokers. The pattern of low capitalization still prevails so that American initiative has produced hordes of small and marginal home builders who cannot take advantage of the economies of large-scale production.

2. *The process of improving the design of American houses and communities will have to be extended.* In recent years the design of houses has been radically changed, but many of the changes are half measures, fads, or in the interests of profit as against consumer bene-

fits. The ideas promulgated by the British garden city planners and rationalized by the Bauhaus school of architects have given an entirely new vista to residential design. But too often the changes have meant only smaller, more glamorous houses with less privacy. Severely functional and collectivist architectural theories have tended to neglect aesthetic values and basic social needs. A well-built home serving the social goals of family and community life must be produced on a large-scale basis, and yet permit the variety and adaptability demanded by the diversity of American life.

3. *The efforts of the government to spur housing improvement through urban renewal and planning programs will have to be carefully weighed and clarified.* In the past, federal and state programs were launched as stop-gap efforts to particular problems which have been shirked in the general housing market. Now the nation's housing policy is one of patchwork programs constantly threatened by the opposition of large groups of citizens who inspire legislative wrecking efforts. The whole new concept of urban renewal is retarded by the ambiguity and the unwieldly character of government participation. The excesses of bureaucracy must be corrected. Care must be taken that agencies, in their zeal for carrying out programs, do not disregard the rights of families. Nevertheless, relocation programs, housing code enforcement and project plans must all be thoughtfully examined in an informed manner, not in a spirit of anti-government hysteria. On the local level lethargy, ineptitude and lack of resolution balk worthy programs. In some areas outmoded city codes and standards prevent community re-

building. The definition of democratic governmental action in housing and urban reform must be comprehensive enough to include federal, state and local roles, but it must also permit maximum flexibility and private initiative.

4. *A popular social formula for the urban renewal process must be achieved.* This formula must evoke private citizen support and guidance and yet allow for shrewd technical supervision of community rebuilding. Such a formula must be genuinely accepted by the private business interests and carefully checked by strong consumer organizations. Urban renewal programs should be operative on a metropolitan basis, going beyond the old city boundaries that are the legacy of horse-and-buggy days. This process will require a massive effort of public education and organization. Our society is quite capable of such an effort. We have developed public support for health reforms, mass education and large-scale consumer services through advertising and promotional campaigns which arose out of social needs. We should use education on a similar scale to build support of urban renewal and reorganization.

The liberty and integrity of our urban social life depend upon a restoration of the civic responsibility which flows from the residential community. A French commentator states that

By their very form, the dwelling, or the collection of houses and services, imposes on the occupant, on the people who live there, a particular employment of their leisure time, even a particular mental outlook. A locality stamped with the marks of human presence inevitably affects the mind with ugliness or beauty. The arrangement of dwelling-houses has also an effect on social relations; it is responsible for fusion or segregation, and can resolve or aggravate the social tensions arising from the necessary conditions of labour and political life. There is no field that calls for more rethinking, in regard to social and psychological complications, than that of housing and town planning.[16]

The way is open for bold and constructive departures.

Within this new urban community the Christian community must find its place. The parish affiliation must be made a living thing for urban Christians. Through social action we must find a way of re-establishing the sense of geographical and functional affinity with the parish unit. Grouping Christian families within the parish into sub-units and working out programs of worship and collaboration for them should strengthen the ties which physical proximity in good neighborhoods can naturally induce. Other parish tactics to deal with the mobility and heterogeneity of urban families are needed. It is only by giving the Christian community stronger focus that a sense of reverent dedication to a particular area can be induced. This dedication can then be projected into community life through the relations of Christians with their non-Christian neighbors.

In the rebuilding of parish life we must avoid confusing the essential sacramental and spiritual purposes of the parish with the worthy, but definitely subordinate, outgrowths of Christian missionary activity. The parish is not a point of reference for all problems. Its role in the community is primarily one of teaching, healing and sanctifying souls, not caring for every local community need. The Christian involvement in the complex community affairs of our cities should, therefore, be conducted through groups that are distinct from the parish, yet benefiting from the life of the spirit developed in the house of the Lord itself.

In the work of addressing urban problems Christians should be eager to experiment. Nobody knows the forms of the new urban order. They must be sought out through investment, community development and private coöperative action. We should not be afraid to make small beginnings in a world of giantism. This approach in no way contradicts the necessity for an intellectual breadth of vision and comprehension. The ideals of graduated activity and an extensive viewpoint complement one another and assure thoroughness in relation to long-range objectives.

In addition to its willingness to experiment, Christian social action in the urban sphere must be based upon a voluntarist and personalist understanding of the urban man's character. This will help to adapt large-scale programs to the individualism of the modern city dweller. It will also guard against the coercion or paternalism of social reformers and technicians. Only by insisting upon personal motivation and responsibility can we hope to arouse the urban people to a spirit of civic pride and ambition and to a development of strong new community forms.

The foregoing paragraphs constitute a program of study, organization, education and social action of Christians in urban affairs. The program is aimed at responding to the trial the modern Christians are subjected to in the revolutionary city. It should be clear to those who make a sincere inquiry into conditions in the urban metropolis that such a Christian intervention is urgently needed.

The Christian seeks nothing less than the adoration of the presence and the love of God in every pulse of the revolutionary city, in its men, in its work and play and in the potential dignity of its extraordinary life. This is the aim of our social striving.

NOTES

1. A. D'Entreves, *Selected Political Writings of St. Thomas* (New York: Oxford University Press, 1948), p. 197.
2. Pope Pius XII, Discourse of October 21, 1947.
3. *Social Justice Statement of the Australian Hierarchy* (Melbourne: Renown Press, Ltd., 1955).
4. Otis D. Duncan, "The Optimum Size of Cities," in *Cities and Society, loc. cit.,* p. 772. W. A. Robson, ed., *Great Cities of the World* (London: George Allen and Unwin, 1954), p. 417. Amos H. Hawley, *The Changing Shape of Metropolitan America* (Glencoe, Illinois: The Free Press, 1955).
5. Colin Clark, "The Economic Functions of the City in Relation to its Size," in *Econometrica* (Vol. XIII), p. 97.
6. For an evaluation of modern urban planning history see "The Utopians," in Arthur B. Gallion *The Urban Pattern* (New York: Van Nostrand Co., 1950).
7. Fred K. Vignam, *The Crisis of the Cities* (Washington, D. C.: Public Affairs Press, 1955), p. 85.
8. *The Exploding Metropolis,* by the editors of *Fortune Magazine* (Garden City: Doubleday and Co., 1958), is a sharply written critique of urban trends that points up the lack of a social policy among government and planning agencies.

9. See Henry Churchill's summary of this failure in *The City is the People* (New York: Reynal and Hitchcock, 1945).

10. See Thomas F. O'Dea in *The Church in the Changing Community* (New York: Fordham University Press, 1957) for the need for religious sociology *vis à vis* urbanism.

11. The Collegium publishes a monthly newsletter which may be obtained by writing to P.O. Box 5188, 216 Patton Avenue, Shreveport, Louisiana.

12. For an account of infant efforts to organize an apostolate specifically in urban affairs see "Housing: Big City Apostolate," by Dennis Clark in *Apostolic Perspectives* (Spring 1957).

13. Rev. François Houtart in *Social Compass*, Vol. II, Nos. 5 and 6.

14. The inclusion of the rural parish in this list is significant, for it has been one effect of modern urbanism to bring about cultural *rapprochement* between the countryside and the city through swift transportation and communication. The society of the future may be technically proficient to such an extent that mechanical methods and organization will be as much a fixture of the rural scene as of the city. This is almost true today on the great corporation farms where much of the food for urban areas is grown. The health and vitality of urban life depend more than ever upon a balanced relationship with rural hinterlands. Without the tempering effects of rural influences, the intensity and regimen of life in the revolutionary city tend to be deeply depressing. On the subject of urban-rural adjustment see W. Frey, C. P. Loomis, and J. A. Beagle, "The Fusion of Urban and Rural" in *Cities and Society, loc. cit.,* p. 214.

15. Pope Pius XII, Address on the Fiftieth Anniversary of *Rerum Novarum, Catholic Mind* (39, 1941), p. 13.

16. André Raillet, *Christianity and Freedom* (New York: The Philosophical Library, 1956), pp. 134-5.

Conclusion

The whole task of analyzing the urban scene and clearly defining the roles of Christian lay leaders, families, parishes, communities and movements in relation to it has only just begun. "The conditions of what is called 'modern civilization' are no longer human," said the late Cardinal Suhard. No other civilization could so truly bear this charge. The urban Christian bears the responsibility of understanding his environment not only in terms of practical plans for physical renewal, but in its philosophical and religious implications.

In attempting to understand the metropolis in philosophical terms, a balance must be maintained which relates the urban problem to the other issues of our times. Above all the problem of urbanism must be seen against the general background of the great modern social revolutions. Although the revolutionary city is the form into which the industrial civilization has organized its social life, the spirit of modern life has been derived from social and philosophical systems. The philosophies which dissolved the Western Christian social ethic in favor of rationalist liberalism and idealistic humanism have appeared bankrupt in the terrible ordeals of the 20th cen-

tury. The prophets of modern scientific progress and
rational transformation have had their social gospels trag-
ically propagated. Comte's religion of humanity, Saint-
Simon's ethic of technology, Hegel's historical rationalism
have been shattered by the totalitarian efforts to trans-
mute such philosophies into social realities.

The Hegelian rationalism which so captivated the 19th
century socialists has been alternately traduced and repudiated by Marxist fanaticism, Nazism and the trend toward irrational statism. Attempts to construct an ethical
foundation for modern life on positivist systems of
thought have produced only a similar philosophy of immediate ends and expedient means.

The philosophical penury of modern social thought is
reflected throughout the realm of social studies. In the
field of urban studies it is unusual for works to include
any serious examination of the fundamental philosophical
issues so vital to the problems of community life. Social
thinkers ignore these issues and content themselves
with an ever more painstaking enumeration of physical
changes. This value-free approach stems much more from
philosophical confusion than from empirical scruple.

The urban society which embodies the revolutionary
social drama of our time has radically altered the character and spirit of every class and institution. The changes
taking place are swift, violent and fundamental. They
have repeatedly altered the basic constitution of society
and the functions of social groups. They have critically
affected personality, family, labor, leisure, worship, and
education. The convulsive process of urban social life
begs for some order, some equilibrium which will temper

and direct its excessive tendencies. Its exploitive ethos, its wasteful giantism, the crudity of its cultural syncretism all demand a remedy. We can admit all of these grave needs, yet we dare not fall into the kind of error which would see in the revolutions of modern times only a negative force. The force is human, obsessive, brilliant, potentially destructive or creative, but neither categorically good nor evil.

The restoration of this order can come about through the prevalence of the valid and realistic concept of man contained in the Christian Gospel. To bring this Gospel to the fore in the urban life centers of modern civilization requires a recasting of traditional forms.

From its foundation Christianity has been a revolutionary social ethic. At the formation of the Church, as Don Luigi Sturzo says, "a religious society took shape which transcended the boundaries of every other society. . . the effects of such an event were bound to be revolutionary."[1] The church, as Cardinal Saliege has said, is the total revolution. It has many times come to grips with evils in society by a kind of internal revolution. Pope Pius XII has put the idea in a contemporary context: "There is running throughout the world an urge for rebirth, a cry of revolution. It will be the Christian Revolution."[2]

Just as Christianity penetrated and subsequently informed and interpreted classical civilization, so must it now transform the technical civilization of modern times. No quality inherent in this new society makes the assertion of spiritual values impossible if they are made relevant to the society and its problems. Here is where the new elite makes its decisions. Here is where the forms of the new society are molded. Here, to the Christian vision, is where Christ, in His people, awaits a Resurrection amid the streets and towers, above the pride and wilfulness of human affairs.

NOTES

1. Don Luigi Sturzo, *The Inner Laws of Society* (New York: P. J. Kenedy and Sons, 1944), p. 82.
2. As quoted in the *New York Times*, March 25, 1957.

Appendix: The Evolution of the City

Modern urbanism presents a unique problem. Its character and the difficulties of the Christian who lives within it will become clearer if we place it in the context of the evolution of the Western city. To see the city as a way of life with a traditionally religious orientation will perhaps give the reader another kind of insight into the peculiar problems facing the urban Christian of the 20th century.

THE ANCIENT CITY

Between 5000 B.C. and 3500 B.C., numerous cities developed in the Nile valley, in the Mesopotamian basin and in Northern India. These cities were formed against a peasant background of agriculture, animal husbandry and domestic crafts. A number of inventions and disciplines gave rise to the cities. To the basic achievement of a reliable food supply were added the arts of metallurgy, writing, commerce and effective government, and there began a kind of social experience radically different from that of the nomad or farmer. By gathering greater numbers of men together for long periods of time, it opened countless possibilities for social interaction and allowed for the specialization and intensification of labor.

Conscious mastery of the basic elements which composed the ancient city developed gradually. Control of the cities in Asia and the Middle East was vested in military and religious despotisms. The temple, the market and the royal residence became the central institutions. But for a view of political institutions vital to the development of Western civilization, one must turn to the experience of the Greeks.

The city became the subject of such astonishing virtuosity in the hands of the Greeks that the Western mind still is fascinated by their achievement. All about the shores of the Eastern Mediterranean and into the interior of Asia the Greeks raised their cities. The Greek empires were an epic of cultural transmission, and the Greek city was the instrument of a remarkably effective imperialism. These cities represented the first clear recognition, as can be seen from Greek political thought and policy, of the social utility and cultural advantages of the urban way of life.

The Greek "polis" and the other ancient cities were religious institutions, representing, in part, a culmination of the social force of pagan beliefs. The physical scene, even in the severe Greek city, was almost always dominated by the temple. The ministrations of government, class and family had both religious meaning and the ritual through which to express it. The officially adopted traditional cults were a clear adjunct of political function and the touchstones of social solidarity and allegiance. The natural group feeling and religious orthodoxy was tolerant to a degree, but really serious competition within the city walls was not accepted. There was a rigidity of official religious outlook which served well in cultural and military colonization and provided a transcendent rationale to set the civilized men apart from the barbarians. This unification of urban order and religious focus would eventually assure the triumph of the city over all other competing forms of community life.

The Romans, although lacking the inventiveness and aesthetic gifts of the Greeks, reënforced the Hellenic achievement with their strong sense of order, their administration and engineering and the sheer vastness of their imperial exertions. Alexandria, Antioch, Constantinople and Corinth added Roman strength to Greek foundations. Roman garrisons and outposts were established along the fertile rim of Africa, across the Danube, up the Rhine and beyond the Pyrenees. The legions marched on the roads they built themselves and struck deep the roots of Pax Romana. In a civilizing process unequalled until modern times, Rome transmitted the city way of life beyond the ancient world into two whole new maritime worlds to the North and West. The spread of Roman centers across central and northern Europe set the initial conditions for the permanent urban settlement of this rich area through the long medieval period.

Standing above this Roman accomplishment, however, was the function performed by Rome herself. Besides being a populous place, a "holy place," as were other ancient centers, Rome was preëminently a political affiliation. The juridical qualities of her life were projected to imperial proportions, so that by legal fiction and juridical fact the entire ancient world could be subsumed into affinity with the City of the Seven Hills. The Greeks presided over a loose hegemony, but the Romans created from their city a lasting political entity. To the notion of "urbs," or place of assembly, was added the ideal of "civitas," a place of radiating civil authority and power. Through this device the city became the archtype and microcosm of the political state. The identification and specification of political authority through urbanism was one of the surpassing attainments of the ancient world. It insured that the struggles of values and ideologies would hinge upon the cities in the West, imparting a vitality and character to the West which contrasted markedly with the temper of oriental societies. The Roman synthesis of formal statecraft and urbanism was only seriously challenged in the West by the agrarian feudalism which was one of the responses to the difficulties of civilizing the European peoples.

If Rome was to conquer through the city, she was also to fall through emergencies complicated by her own urban giantism. At the very heart of the empire the restless populace of "the eternal City" began to exercise a treacherous tyranny over the proud senate and tribunes. As the population increased, the diseases of apathy, cynicism and selfish aggrandizement grew, corroding the quality of government and undermining the hardihood of outlook which was the strongest weapon of the legions. The most critical circumstance speeding Rome's decline, however, was the imbalance between the urban centers which were Rome's glory and the rural areas from which she drew her traditional vigor. As Christopher Dawson has said:

All this brilliant expansion of urban civilization had in it the seeds of its own decline. It was essentially the civilization of a leisured class, the urban bourgeoisie and their dependents, and though the process of urbanization promoted the advance of civilization, it also involved a vast increase in unproductive expenditure and a growing strain on the resources of the empire . . . The population of Italy and of the more Romanized provinces grew steadily more unsuitable for military service . . . The old opposition between the city, state and the mercenary army, between the ideals of citizenship and military despotism . . . now reappeared in a more serious form than ever before and destroyed the social balance of the imperial system.[1]

By the time St. Augustine was writing his *City of God* little more was left of the real substance of the imperial cities than the old titles and forms. The social content of these monumental centers had been dissipated in repeated alarms and reverses. Barbarian war lords replaced the tribunes and used vulgarized Roman modes of control as they saw fit.

In this world of confusion and anarchy, the vital faith and institutions of the Christians seemed to many to offer order and hope. "We are of yesterday," said Tertullian, "and we have filled every place belonging to you; cities, islands, fortresses, towns, assemblies, even the camps, your tribes, your electoral divisions, the palace, the Senate, the law courts; the only thing we have left to you for yourselves is your temples!"

Christian beliefs began to work amid the broken Roman order. The revelation of Christ thrust to the very essence of life and gradually reshaped the mind and ways of the ancient world. The way of Christ had implications for the entire realm of authority, the state, the family, the community, the slave world—even the world of the barbarian. "The world was recast, in intent and in execution . . . the world mission of the Church was established for all time in the great urban centers of the ancient world . . . among the international lower middle class population of the great cities—shopkeepers, artisans, merchants, slaves and freemen of the great houses. It was in this uprooted, denationalized, cosmopolitan population that the spiritual need was greatest and that the word was most eagerly heard and accepted."[2]

The cities of Jerusalem, Antioch, Constantinople, Alexandria and Rome became flourishing centers of Christian life. And in every city of the old empire a new citizen body grew up, the "plebs Christi." As the dignitaries and functions of the old order declined, the authority of the new dispensation grew. Eventually the bishop became the chief dignitary of the city. The Christian influence penetrated law and custom, and Christian leaders took the initiative. Everywhere in the old Empire the Roman usages were transformed into Christian ones, and the imperial forms became the vehicles for the dissemination of the new way of life.

Christianization was a gradual process because it was pledged to a total ideal. The vision was universal; no phase of life was exempt. The standards did not admit of easy compromise. Its theological propositions were debated with inexorable energy; its ethics, refined. But the God-centered view of life proposed by Christianity could not rapidly stabilize the institutional vertigo of the Graeco-Roman heritage.

In the great centers of the Eastern Empire, where society was less fluid, a long respite was won, but in the 7th century the Mohammedan challenge weakened the Byzantine world, and the Christian mission labored to maintain its independence. The political mantle of the Eastern Caesars was wrapped about with the cope of Byzantine ecclesiastical life, and the social body sank beneath the dual responsibility.

The Western experience was one of painstaking reconstruction. The evangelization of the dominant barbarian peoples was slow, not only because of the vastness of the task, but also because of the nature of Christianity itself. The recession of Roman influence had been physical as well as spiritual. The great Roman engineering works ceased to function; aqueduct and bath, fortress and forum fell into disuse, and the Goth pillaged stone for his first constructions from the roads which had borne the might of the Caesars.

Even the very land seemed to testify to the absence of adequate control. Montalembert speaks of the unrestrained growth of the great forests:

These new forests extended by degrees to the immense clumps of dark and impenetrable woods, which had always covered a considerable part of Gaul. . . . The intermediate regions between the great forests and the fields, between the mountains and the cultivated plains, were with too much justice entitled deserts, because the population had abandoned them till the monks brought back fertility and life. We must imagine Gaul and all the neighboring countries, the whole extent of France, Switzerland, Belgium, and both banks of the Rhine—that is to say the richest and most populous countries of modern Europe

—covered with forests such as are scarcely to be seen in America, and of which there does not now remain the slightest trace in the old world.[3]

The social initiative characteristic of Western Christianity operated in this wilderness as well. Leading the advance were the communal monastic settlements. They did not advance as the Romans had, with the momentum of a temporal empire behind them. The monk "came out of a devastated, decrepit and powerless old world, to plunge into the unknown . . . without arms, without sufficient implements, and often without a single companion. . . . But he bore with him a strength that nothing has ever surpassed or equalled, the strength conferred by faith in a living God . . . by contempt of all material joy and by an exclusive devotion to the spiritual and future life. He thus advanced, undaunted and serene; and often without thinking what he did, he opened a road to all the benefits of agriculture, labor and Christian civilization."[4]

This description probably appears reasonable only to those who have some understanding of the tremendous potency and élan of the monastic ideal. Modern authorities on urban history have agreed, however, in an unreserved admiration for the achievement of the early Western monastics who drained, cleared and built wherever they moved. Each monastery was like a small town in design. Through these settlements the basis for stable urban life was re-established. "The monks with unceasing energy created conditions for civilization everywhere. . . . Their work cannot be overestimated."[5]

As civilized city life was rebuilt, the contrast between

the new and the ancient attitudes became actualized. Christianity represented a liberation from the cultural and political rigidity of the ancient urban systems. Fustel de Coulanges discusses the antipathy of the ancient city for the "stranger."[6] The spirit of Christianity can be seen if we contrast St. Paul's instruction on hospitality and the parable of the good Samaritan with the civic hostility of the ancient city. The medieval city became more a "confluence" and less of a rigid rampart or a conscious "agency" than the ancient city. By inheriting the Roman administrative forms the liberating spirit of the Christian way was communicated, and yet the Roman concept of "city" as a juridical and political entity survived. To these concepts were added the "holy government" of the "people of God" and the new institutions of the developing medieval society.

THE MEDIEVAL CITY

The medieval city was a fusion of Roman influence, monastic activity, popular Catholic religious institutions and Gothic innovations. The culture which animated it was a "folk culture." Guild and commune, cathedral and university, were institutions of the people in a broad but immediate sense. The medieval city was strongly influenced by the rural feudal background from which it arose, was much more a product of military truce than was the ancient city, and was a city of relatively free men, as compared to the ancient slave-serviced cities of the classical world. These features made its atmosphere much more expansive than that of the ancient cities. The rural conditioning produced a flexible and organic relationship between topography and buildings. "The medieval town was like an ornamental pattern of man's art fitted into the majestic environment of nature's art," says Saarinen.[7]

Thus in the medieval cities the majority of inhabitants were free. The economic revival in the Mediterranean after the Dark Ages and the commerce of such combinations of cities as the Hanseatic League capitalized on the venturesome spirit of the burgher freemen. The independent, voluntary guild and communal life which flourished under religious protection was quick to defend itself against the political state. Whereas the ancient city was the state and was inextricably bound to imperial ambitions, the medieval city consistently fought the state and contested the pretensions of the larger sovereignties and royal regimes.

Saarinen has called this kind of religiously dominated folk city "a genuine expression of the best aspirations of the population."[8] It cannot be doubted that the harmonization of the diversities of European life was only made possible by the elastic, yet controlled, Christian dialectic. The fact that the Christianization of Europe corresponded with the urban settlement of the Continent set conditions for the cultural eminence and prerogative which Europe enjoyed for centuries.

Modern scholarship has reversed the prejudiced judgments of the 18th and 19th century historians to reveal medieval life as one of the great creative syntheses. The city building which gave to Europe its centers of civilization was a process influenced by an active religious spirit.

THE RENAISSANCE CITY

The Renaissance and the Protestant Reformation disrupted the religious and social ideology on which the medieval system rested. The social rupture of Europe, described by Lewis Mumford as the "analytical decomposition of the Church," resulted in a subversion of the medieval city. New trade, new ideas and new necessities brought an abandonment of what were often ossified patterns.

The great social changes which accompanied the passing of medievalism were eventually to have an explosive effect upon the city. Arnold Toynbee, R. H. Tawney, Max Weber and others have analyzed how religious revisions were reflected in the "modern" attitude towards the world's goods. Reformation and counter-Reformation, exploration and mercantilism, the nation state and dynastic imperialism ushered in an age when man acquired a growing control over material life; this material control induced a superficial assurance, and the old primacy of spiritual discernment and qualification was no longer as operative a principle.

The classical forms of the ancient cities were rediscovered and inspired a building revival based on the architecture of the Greek and Roman world. Princely families vied with one another in the magnificence of their subsidies for re-creations of classical artistry. Brilliant guilds of artisans and craftsmen competed to adorn the palaces, the churches and the squares with surpassing skill. The Roman author Vitruvius became the god of Renaissance planners; his *De Architectura* was reproduced in faithful and spurious editions with many popular commentaries. During the Renaissance, the planning of the city became once again a clearly civic function, and less of a function of royal service or folk development. The higher rationality of the ancient architect reasserted itself and the trade centers of Italy and France in a great dream of imitation and aspiration reënacted the execution of the classical aesthetic.

THE INDUSTRIAL CITY

The inventions of the 17th and 18th centuries led to diligent expansion of extractive economic activities. Forests were invaded, mountains were explored, and the metals and fluids of the earth adventurously and methodically captured and refined. This process was carried on at a phenomenal rate in the 19th century. With materials available in abundance, the process of fabricating them became rationalized, and productive enterprises were formulated into the factory system. Concomitant with the growth of factories was the revolution in transportation. The changes in transportation made accessible both more materials and markets, and the outpouring bounty of the new economic system became a continual reaction stimulus which spurred the industrial revolution to repeated successes. Nature yielded marvels under the industrial system, and cities as men had known them were rapidly elected as workshops of science and industry without special accommodations.

The effects of the factory economy on rural areas which

had previously so strongly conditioned social life were radical and debilitating. From the weakening of ruralism was drawn the strength of the factory-breeding cities:

All over the civilized globe the rural regions lay under a cloud—in Great Britain, France, Germany, Russia, Italy, Belgium. The introduction of farm machinery and the opening up of virgin fields in the Argentine and Australia added to those of the American West, rendered unprofitable much of the agricultural labor of the Old World, stirred rural conservatism into fierce discontent and enhanced the attractions of the nearby city for the peasant toilers. Everywhere there was an exodus from the soil while the trading and industrial centers waxed by leaps and bounds. Between 1881 and 1891 Prussia added two million to her cities while her countryside barely increased half a million; rural France lost a half million at the same time her urban places gained well over a million; the rural population of England and Wales declined over two hundred thousand, while the towns and cities advanced by three and a quarter million. By 1891 London and Paris had doubled their population of mid-century and Berlin had more than quadrupled hers.[9]

This extraordinary augmentation of the old towns and urban centers continued at an accelerating pace into the 20th century and has not abated.

Such a vast human congregation could not have taken place on the basis of scientific and economic rationale alone. The ideals and orientations of the leaders and participants in this movement facilitated the changes which filled the cities with engines and smoke. The centuries which witnessed the transition also gave rise to vigorous liberal and revolutionary political movements.

As Crane Brinton shows so well in his *Ideas and Men*,

beginning with the Enlightenment of the 18th century a new cosmology as well as a powerful personalized motivation was conceived as the basis for social effort:

The Enlightenment promised heaven on earth, soon, and by a process that meant for the individual a "natural" release of expansive, appetitive forces within himself, not self-denial and inner discipline . . . it is clear that the ordinary educated person—and by the late nineteenth century there were millions of them in the Western world—had in the hundred years that followed the American and French revolutions changed his intellectual garments considerably. . . . Indeed, all over the Western world men took it for granted that enterprise and invention would produce ever more and more conveniences. . . . The romantic and idealistic elements in the nineteenth century revulsion from the eighteenth ought in strict logic, perhaps, to have made optimistic belief in human perfectibility impossible. Some did draw such consequences from the revolt against the age of prose and reason. But the man in the street did not.[10]

Enthusiastic popular belief in the idea of Progress underlay the application of scientific knowledge to bring about material improvement. The formal philosophical systems of rationalism, idealism, utilitarianism, pragmatism and positivism expressed the same conviction and were regarded as descriptions of what already existed or at least as pale reflections of the actual force of scientism and popular optimism. With the enfranchisement of the general populations of the Western nations, these sentiments became the controlling assumptions of public policy as well.

The fusion of scientific capability and the optimistic

"zeitgeist" of social liberation interacted with a third great movement transforming the old Christendom. Nationalism, the expansion and idealization of the political state, changed the countries of Europe and the New World from loose federations and hegemonies into ever more tightly knit organizations. Old allegiances were exploited, new state functions were discovered and political power became more and more centralized. Governments concerned themselves intensively with economic life and gained control over the resources of their territories. The court cities of the early nation state gave way to the wealth producing industrial centers which made nations into first-class powers. The industrial cities became the most carefully guarded prizes of the militarism which was to wrack Europe in the 20th century.

The nationalism which activated the centralized modern political states had to struggle against old forms and power elements which refused to commit industrial resources to the government, but the state won control through intervention in times of economic crisis and military danger. Not only was the dominant interest of the industrial city identified with the national interest, but the attitudes of the industrial urban milieu eliminated old elements of the national culture. Thus, the remains of feudalism, the agrarian folk cultures and ancient regional divisions were superseded or made meaningless in the new politically guided order of things.

Another phenomenon in the rise of modern urbanism, partly cause and partly effect, was the tremendous growth in population which took place beginning in the 17th century. Advances in medicine, nutrition, and hygiene have spread throughout the world under Western influence and spurred this rise. Concurrently, the new mobility of the greatly increased populations of Western Europe affected in a fundamental way their internal development. A partitioning of urban life took place on an ethnic and class basis which vitiated comprehensive control of the environment.

The ascendancy of the industrial city has imposed upon modern life the regimentation of the technological order. Manchester, the first great industrial city, rose by virtue of such a system:

In contrast to the discipline of custom, tradition and force of pre-industrial society, the basic social control in early Manchester was regimentation; not regimentation by order supported by force, but regimentation developing under the integrating power of the urban milieu. The factory enforced a system of management through a routine of work and a minute division of labor. The codes and fines were incidental aids to support this regime, and in time they became unnecessary. The cheap press and new forms of recreation organized pervasive standardizations of belief and emotion. Since the accommodation of the most families in the least space was the governing principle of the jerry-builders unalterable architecture—rows of apartment houses, back to back, with two rooms upstairs and two rooms down—the working class residential areas were models of physical uniformity. It was, however, no greater than the uniformity that pervaded working class life as a whole. The source of this regimentation was the industrial process itself and the interests of the entrepreneurial class, to which, in fact the economy of uniformity was essential.[11]

Although the industrialized city imposed a new system upon social processes, the immensely complex proliferation of the new urbanism permitted the growth of distinctive types of cities. The new system could be used in many ways. There were cities based on productive specializations—oil cities and centers for textiles, for example. Industrial cities took lines of development conditioned by location, politics and social accidents, as cities have always done. But, wherever the modern centers grew, they grew with the accompaniment of technology, corporate manufacturing enterprise and the doctrines of social liberalism. The dominant interests of the industrial city dictated the physical arrangement of the community, acting in terms of its economic needs and its avid faith in the righteousness of its social goals.

Thus a unity was created for the city, but it was a mechanical unity which overrode the subtleties and recondite considerations of organic social life. A servile proletariat, without traditions, skills or cohesion was exploited —practically as a marketable commodity—in the "insensate industrial town." The industrial Leviathan was built upon the suffering of the rootless, dispossessed masses. In an ironic paradox, the system bound its "wage slaves" by a promise of its own benevolence, a promise made credible despite bitter contradictions by occasional material rewards.

The persistence of the expoitation of industrial workers and the miserable state of their living conditions caused a violent reaction which sought, often in an agony of blind protest, to bring about something resembling social solidarity for the toiling stepchildren of the industrial cities. This reaction took its most notable form in the Marxist socialist movement.

This movement foresees a redeeming new order and

has spoken to the oppressed urban poor in terms which it understands—the terms of material deliverance and temporal fulfillment. Having served a system of practical production for immediate material ends, the urban proletariat has become imbued with a materialist outlook, even in the class war for its own "liberation." The social solidarity and humanitarian salvation yearned for by Marxism is to be founded on the dynamic of material progress which has been the ethos of the industrial city. The scientism which is so characteristic of modern urban achievement is idolized, and "scientific materialism" is applied to history and politics as an all-embracing interpretive mystique.

Marxism, because it was born of industrialism, is conversant with all of the causal factors of industrial urbanism. It comprehends these factors, but it has given little evidence that Marxist "reform" will produce anything more than a centralized version of the old environmental despotism. Scientism, mass political jingoism, and the superstitions of continual materialist progress are all retained in the Marxist program. The terror-ridden history of Marxian socialism can only testify to the tragic inability of this movement to deal with the social problems synthesized in the industrial city.

The secular, bureaucratic "welfare state" also resulted from agitation for some kind of ameliorating control over exploitive productive systems. The political imposition of partial controls, which often served to compound confusion, was justified by a bloc of effective opinion which criticized scientific achievement in bitterly trenchant terms. Sidney Webb wrote: "If to ameliorate the human lot in life had been any part of the purpose of the great mechanical inventions or of the far-reaching discoveries of physical science of the preceding half century (before 1842) they must be accounted to have egregiously failed."[12]

Such reform opinion provided the basis for governmental intervention for social reform which has become continuous in the welfare states. The efforts of Scandinavia, England and the West European countries to guide economic development and restore integrity to city life are still in process. The compatibility of liberal democratic social freedom with the need for social controls is the question at issue throughout the urbanized West in country after country.

In addition to these political reactions to the phenomena of industrial urbanism there occurred throughout the 19th century a series of utopian experiments, abetted by intellectual and literary romanticism which sought to discover a way of life that would preserve men from the denigrations of slum conditions and mechanized servitude. Philosophical radicalism and religious subjectivism motivated leaders to found new communities. Three hundred such religious or utopian communities were set up in 19th century America, varying widely in their aims and justification. Many of the communities were not directed toward social reconstruction at all, but were islands of protest or retreats where harried religious sects could exercise their beliefs freely.

Experiments such as these and the disenchantment with the new environment of influential intellectuals such as Ruskin, Thoreau and Tolstoy helped to create a ferment

of liberal humanitarian concern. The theory of uninter-
rupted human progress was no longer so generally held.
Men pored over biological data and evolutionary theories
which hinted at mysterious relationships between man
and nature. The coöperative aspects of religion began
once more to receive the attention which had long been
diverted by religious strife. All of these developments
formed a pattern of social re-examination which shook
the assurance of the builders of the industrial city.

What was the response of the churches? Ostensibly
these institutions represented a resource of social philosophy and initiative which could be expected to react
strongly to such extensive environmental changes. It is
true that there were many responses from religious groups.
Whatever may have been the role of the Protestant ethic
in fostering the rise of industrialism, many expressions of
protest against social irresponsibility were contributed by
19th century Protestantism. The evangelization of poor
populations, the zeal for reform culminating in labor
parties in several countries, and such programs as the Salvation Army and the Settlement House movement gave
testimony to the vitality of Protestant and "free church"
communions.

The exertion of Protestant opinion for reform and humane standards in the new urban environment, however,
was compromised by weaknesses in the Protestant system
itself. In an age of growing centralization the Protestant
denominations were completing a cycle of decentralization. The fragmentation of spiritual opinion which they
represented prevented a marshalling of sufficient strength
to contend with the corporate empires or the national

states which coveted them. Indeed, in many places the state churches were wedded to the political tolerance of industrial irresponsibility.

Because of their diversity, community controls under Protestant religious auspices became less and less effective. The structure and sources of community entities became blurred, and the secularization of community ideals was hastened. A broad philosophical design for communal forms, whether economic, residential, or cultural, was lacking. The breadth of common commitment required for cohesive association was made impossible because of the Protestant individualist interpretation of life's most fundamental issues. At times Protestantism acted as the actual agent which dissolved community bonds and usages. Transitory utopian experiments and strongly personalist witnesses given amid the disorder of the 19th century slum cities were not enough to provide social governance for a headlong and often ruthless urbanization.

Because of the inherently divided and individualistic character of Protestantism, it would seem that its major contribution to the social control of modern city forms must of necessity be under a humanitarian aegis which is not formally religious.

The Catholic Church during the rise of the industrial cities was effectively exiled from the councils of social decision where urbanism was most advanced. The Protestant Revolt had shattered the social supremacy that Catholicism had maintained in Europe. The popular folk cultures, so strongly informed by Catholicism, were in recession. Political revolutions deposed one Catholic establishment after another and broke up the monastic and university institutions through which the Church had exercised widespread influence.

The Catholic response to this organized hostility against it had two succeeding waves of effort. The first was the Counter-Reformation. It was a movement of internal reform and missionary activity. It had as one of its features the support of the Catholic monarchies. While great works of doctrinal refinement, educational activity and missionary zeal were accomplished, the emergent forces which were to shape the modern city were not brought within the ambit of Catholic principles. The attempt to restore the religious unity to European society failed, and the Church in many countries entered a period of harassment and intermittent persecution.

The second phase of Catholic effort began in the latter part of the last century. "With the election of [Pope] Leo XIII, on February 20, 1878, a new age—as it is now universally realized—began in the Church's history. . . . It was a leading principle of Leo XIII's long reign . . . that the Church should never allow itself to be isolated from the general life of the time. . . ."[13] An invigorated Papacy, casting off the last entanglements with lingering feudal ways, charted an earnest and successful course in international affairs. A modus vivendi with the secular liberal democracies was slowly achieved, and the Catholic Church won limited freedom to develop its institutional life, although at times against anti-clerical and militantly anti-Catholic opposition. The great migrations of the 19th century moved millions of Catholics from traditionally Catholic rural settings into the growing cities. The position and sufferings of these masses of people in the urban laboring classes summoned the attention of the modern Popes to the problems of industrialism. In comprehensive terms Papal pronouncements analyzed the fundamental features of industrial life.

The Papal encyclicals *Rerum Novarum* and *Quadregesimo Anno* provided the basis for the development of a modern Catholic social movement aimed at the renovation of life in the most fundamental sense. Liturgical reform, the re-establishment of the great religious orders and the building of a widespread educational and university system gave Catholicism the means partially to carry out a movement for social renewal. But the inroads of the secular outlook were deep and the momentum of the modern social milieu tremendous. Only by activating large segments of the laity in coördinated fashion could Catholics, who were now a practical minority in many strategic places, hope to make an impress in modern affairs. The training and organization of this lay leadership is one of the major concerns of the church in the world of the second industrial revolution.

NOTES

1. Christopher Dawson, *The Making of Europe* (New York: Sheed and Ward, 1952): Meridian Books edition (New York, 1956), pp. 33-34.
2. Christopher Dawson, "Christianity and the Oriental Cultures," *The Commonweal* (November 30, 1957).
3. Charles René Montelambert in "St. Columba," from *The Monks of the West* (St. Columban, Nebraska: The Society of St. Columba, 1927), pp. 8-9.
4. *Ibid.*, p. 10.

5. L. Hilberseimer, *The Nature of Cities* (Chicago: Paul Theobold Co., 1955), p. 84.

6. Fustel de Coulanges, *The Ancient City* (Garden City: Doubleday Anchor Books, 1956), p. 193.

7. Eliel Saarinen, *The City* (New York: Reinhold Publishing Co., 1943), p. 64.

8. *Ibid.*, p. 73.

9. Arthur M. Schlesinger, *The Rise of the City* (New York: Macmillan Co., 1933), p. 79.

10. Crane Brinton, *Ideas and Men* (New York: Prentice-Hall, 1950), p. 408.

11. Leon S. Marshall, "The Emergence of the First Industrial City," in *Cultural Approaches to History* (New York: Columbia University Press, 1940), p. 158.

12. Sidney Webb, "Social Movements," Chapter XXII, *Cambridge Modern History* (Cambridge University Press), p. 731.

13. Philip Hughes, *A Popular History of the Church* (New York: Macmillan Co., 1949), p. 245; pp. 254-255.

BIBLIOGRAPHICAL NOTE

For the reader who is interested in a more detailed treatment of the developments sketched in the Appendix, the following works are suggested. The reader is also referred to the general bibliography.

Baumer, F. L., *Main Currents in Modern Thought* (New York: Alfred Knopf, 1952), Part II.

Dawson, Christopher, *Religion and the Rise of Western Culture* (New York: Sheed and Ward, 1950).

Frankfort, H., and others, *Before Philosophy* (Harmondsworth, England: Penguin Books, 1951).

Giedion, S., *Space, Time and Architecture* (Cambridge: Harvard University Press, 1954).

Gilmore, H. W., *Transportation and the Growth of Cities* (Glencoe, Illinois: The Free Press, 1953).

Glotz, Gustav, *The Greek City and its Institutions* (London: Kegan Paul, Trench, Trubner and Co., 1929).

Hauser, Arnold, *The Social History of Art* (New York: Vintage Books, 1957).

Hayes, C. J. H., *Essays on Nationalism* (New York: Macmillan Co., 1926).

Hiorns, F., *Town Building in History* (London: C. Harrap and Co., 1956).

Lebreton, J. and Zeiller, J., *The History of the Primitive Church* (New York: Macmillan Co., 1944).

Mumford, Lewis, *The Culture of Cities* (New York: Harcourt, Brace and Co., 1938).

Mundy, J. H. and Reisenberg, P., *The Medieval Town* (New York: Van Nostrand Co., 1958).

Palanque, F., and others, *The Church in the Christian Roman Empire*, 2 vols. (New York: Macmillan Co., 1953).

Pirenne, Henri, *Medieval Cities* (Garden City: Doubleday Anchor Books, 1956).

Tunnard, Christopher, "Fire on the Prairies," in *The City of Man* (New York: Charles Scribner's Sons, 1953).

Various authors, *The Ideas and Beliefs of the Victorians* (London: Sylvan Press, 1949).

Wolf, A., *The History of Science, Technology and Philosophy in the Sixteenth and Seventeenth Centuries* (London: G. Allen, 1952).

Bibliography

Alexandersson, G., *The Industrial Structure of American Cities* (Lincoln, Nebraska: University of Nebraska Press, 1956).

Beaver, G., *Christ and Community* (New York: Association Press, 1950).

Bell, B. I., *Crowd Culture* (Chicago: Henry Regnery Co., 1952).

Beyer, G., *Housing—a Factual Analysis* (New York: Macmillan, 1958).

Bogue, D., *The Structure of the Metropolitan Community* (Ann Arbor: University of Michigan Press, 1950).

Botkin, B. A., *Sidewalks of America* (New York: Bobbs-Merrill Co., 1954).

Brinton, C., *Ideas and Men* (New York: Prentice-Hall Co., 1950).

Clark, J. M., *Economic Institutions and Human Welfare* (New York: Alfred Knopf and Co., 1957).

Coulanges, F. de, *The Ancient City* (Garden City: Doubleday Anchor Books, 1956).

Dawson, C., *Religion and the Rise of Western Culture* (New York: Sheed and Ward, 1950).

Dobriner, W., *The Suburban Community* (New York: G. Putnam and Sons, 1958).

Drucker, P., *The Future of Industrial Man* (New York: John Day Co., 1942).

Fichter, J., *Social Relations in the Urban Parish* (Chicago: University of Chicago Press, 1954).

Fisher, R. M., *The Metropolis in Modern Life* (Garden City: Doubleday, 1955).

Fogarty, M., *Christian Democracy in Western Europe—1850-1950* (South Bend, Indiana: University of Notre Dame Press, 1957).

Fortune, Editors of, *The Exploding Metropolis* (Garden City: Doubleday and Co., 1958).

Fraigneux, M., *Christianity Is Revolutionary* (Westminster, Maryland: Newman Press, 1955).

Gallion, A. B., *The Urban Pattern* (New York: Van Nostrand Co., 1950).

Geddes, P., *Cities in Evolution* (London: Williams and Newgate, 1949).

Giedion, S., *Space, Time, and Architecture* (Cambridge: Harvard University Press, 1954).

Gist, N. P., and Halbert, L. A., *Urban Society* (New York: Crowell Co., 1948).

Green, C., *American Cities in the Growth of the Nation* (Welwyn, England: John de Graef, 1957).

Gutkind, E. A., *Revolution of Environment* (London: Routledge, Kegan Paul, Ltd., 1957).

Hallowell, J. H., *Main Currents in Modern Political Thought* (New York: Henry Holt and Co., 1950).

Handlin, O., *The Uprooted* (Boston: Little, Brown and Co., 1951).

Hatt, P. and Reiss, A., *Cities and Society* (Glencoe, Illinois: The Free Press, 1957).

Hawley, A., *The Changing Shape of Metropolitan America* (Glencoe, Illinois: The Free Press, 1955).

Hilberseimer, L., *The Nature of Cities* (Chicago: Paul Theobold Co., 1955).

Hiorns, F., *Town Building in History* (London: C. Harrap and Co., Ltd., 1956).

Hitchcock, H. R., *Architecture: 19th and 20th Centuries* (Baltimore: Penguin Books, n.d.).

Liao, Wen Kwei, *The Individual and the Community* (New York: Harcourt Brace Co., 1933).

Marcel, G., *Man Against Mass Society* (Chicago: Henry Regnery Co., 1952).

Mayo, E., *Social Problems of Industrial Civilization* (Cambridge: Harvard University Press, 1946).

Mead, M., *Cultural Values and Technical Change* (New York: Mentor Books, 1957).

Miller, K. D., *Man and God in the City* (New York: Friendship Press, 1954).

Mounier, E., *The Character of Man* (New York: Harper and Brothers, 1956).

Mumford, L., *The Culture of Cities* (New York: Harcourt Brace Co., 1938).

Nef, J. U., *The Cultural Foundations of Industrial Civilization* (Cambridge: Cambridge University Press, 1957).

Nimkoff, M., *Technology and Social Change* (New York: Appleton-Century-Crofts, 1957).

Nisbet, R., *The Quest For Community* (New York: Oxford University Press, 1953).

Nuesse, C. J., and Harte, T. J., *The Sociology of the Parish* (Milwaukee: Bruce Publishing Co., 1951).

Ortega y Gasset, J., *The Revolt of the Masses* (New York: W. W. Norton Co., 1932).

Owen, W., *Cities in the Motor Age* (New York: Association Press, 1950).

Park, R. E. and Burgess, E. W. and McKenzie, R. D., *The City* (Chicago: University of Chicago Press, 1925).

Pirenne, H., *Medieval Cities* (Garden City: Doubleday Anchor Books, 1957).

Queen, S. and Carpenter, D. B., *The American City* (New York: McGraw-Hill Book Co., 1953).

Raillet, A., *Christianity and Freedom* (New York: Philosophical Library, 1956).

Robson, W. A., ed., *Great Cities of the World* (London: George Allen and Unwin, 1954).

Saarinen, E., *The City* (New York: Reinhold Publishing Co., 1943).

Salomon, A., *The Tyranny of Progress* (New York: The Noonday Press, 1955).

Sanders, I. T., *The Community* (New York: Ronald Press, 1958).

Schlesinger, A., *The Rise of the City* (New York: Macmillan Co., 1933).

Self, P., *Cities in Flood* (London: Faber and Faber, Ltd., 1957).

Sert, J. L., *Can Our Cities Survive* (Cambridge: Harvard University Press, 1942).

Spicer, E. H., *Human Problems and Technological Change* (New York: Russell Sage Foundation, 1952).

Suhard, E. Cardinal, *Growth or Decline* (Chicago: Fides Publishers, 1950).

Tunnard, C., *The City of Man* (New York: Charles Scribner's Sons, 1953).

Turner, R., *The Great Cultural Traditions*, vol. 1, *The Ancient Cities* (New York: McGraw-Hill Book Co., 1941).

UNESCO, *Social Implications of Industrialization of Africa South of the Sahara* (1956).

Various authors, *The Church in the Changing Community* (New York: Fordham University Press, 1957).

Various authors, *The Suburban Community* (New York: G. P. Putnam's Sons, 1958).

Vigman, F. K., *The Crisis of the Cities* (Washington: Public Affairs Press, 1955).

Walker, M., *Urban Blight and Slums* (Cambridge: Harvard University Press, 1938).

Webster, D. H., *Urban Planning and Municipal Public Policy* (New York: Harper and Brothers, 1958).

Wirth, L., *Community Life and Social Policy* (Chicago: University of Chicago Press, 1956).

Wolf, A., *The History of Science, Technology and Philosophy in the 16th and 17th Centuries* (London: G. Allen, 1952).

Woodbury, C., *The Future of Cities and Urban Redevelopment* (Chicago: University of Chicago Press, 1953).

Wright, F. L., *The Living City* (New York: Horizon Press, 1959).

Zimmerman, C., *The Family and Civilization* (New York: Harper and Brothers, 1947).